Foreword   **Eleni Papazoglou**
Everything Must Go

Friendly Exchanges   **Lucy Cowling**

New Old Stock (NOS)

Everything Must Go

The Commodity and the Exhibition	Joshua Simon	43
		44
		45
		46
Everything Must Go		47
		48
Changing Display	Lisa Sudhibhasilp	49
		50
		51
Everything Must Go		52
Bag and Bootleg	Elaine M L Tam	53
		54
		55
Everything Must Go		56
Our Range	Eleni Papazoglou	57
	Edited by Daniel Fletcher	58
		59
		60
		61
		62
		63
		64
		65
		66
		67
		68
		69
		70
		71
		72
		73
		74
		75
		76
		77
		78
		79
		80
		81
		82
		83
		84

	85
	86
	87
	88
	89
	90
	91
	92
	93
	94
	95
	96
Everything Must Go	97
	98
	99
	100
Acknowledgements	101
	102
Biographies	103
Colophon	104

Products & Services
Eleni Papazoglou
Foolscap Editions
978-1-7392095-5-1

Foreword

Eleni Papazoglou

A catalogue, a hand book, a manual. An index, a guide, a companion. How is one to deal with the hoard of the world otherwise? Courgettes, tahini, sharp knives, children's scissors, anti-slip bathmats, non-smell wall paint, bargain hand tools, party decorations, durable baskets, bio-laundry powder, 2 for 1 plates, small scale storage solutions, screws in all sizes, electronics made easy, fruity vapes, and forgotten Christmas trees at bargain prices.

Their physical enormity is blurring into one huge lump, oozing excess in bold and italics. Diagonally stacked reds and blues in stripes. A constellation of fluorescent explosions bearing the latest offers floats in a world coated in polythene. The hoard is *carried*: by cardboard boxes, modular hook systems and vacuum formed shells. It is announced by graphics and validated by barcodes. Originals ubiquitous and universal bootlegs are actualised as commodities through the mechanisms of display.[1]

Science fiction writer Ursula K. Le Guin argues that our ancestors' greatest invention was the container:[2] the recipient, the holder.[3] The device that bears [all that is] value in a non-committal entanglement. In this spinning sting, Le Guin's sacred vessel has turned mass produced, surplus and single-use. It is designed, from its inception, to become a container without contents; a bling that lands in the bin just after it convinces one of its commodified truth. Still shining: left behind treasure, redundant—and free!

What if a means is an end? Finally allowed to be its own thing,[4] the container's functional condition collapses into another; that of being not just a system, but a meaning.[5] Not unlike matter, meaning is sought after, found, negotiated, shared, stolen, cherished. It forms anew through gestures — some pertinent and others absurd — taking place in a world adjacent to that of its prior circumstance.

Products & Services is a poetic catalogue of the visual and material languages surrounding commodities. This exploration started as a process of packaging artworks[6] — as to not get damaged while in transport or storage. Eventually, the protective wrapping became their permanent skin and was exhibited as part of them.[7] And as, the only criterion of an act is its elegance,[8] encased works were adorned with phoney equivalents of the ever so familiar trademarks that turn an object into an item of desire. Such were integrated with personal information like social security numbers, and incantations regarding notions of labour and aspirations of high performance. In this process, commercial and art objects were churned together — if, that is to say, they were ever separate. Simultaneously, the act of making turned imposter's play: pastiching the symbolism of retail became an act of self validation. A coping mechanism — part sincere and part ironic — for engaging in clumsy, creative labour that is incompatible with the dominant logics of profit margins and capital gains.[9]

It is impossible to package something without thinking of the moment of unwrapping.[10] It is equally unfeasible to do so without a customer profile. Who is the receiver and what do they want? In conversation, a friend mentioned that the best way to make an artwork is to design for an audience of [a loved] one.[11] Under this premise, creating a product, artistic or otherwise, is putting forward a relationship and thus, offering a part of oneself.[12] To offer is a desire defined as the express readiness to do something for, or, on behalf of someone;[13] an act of service. The term has been used to describe both love languages and industries, and sits queerly between two.

A catalogue, a hand book, a manual. An index, a guide, a companion. *Products & Services*, at times systematic and at others incongruous, takes stock of the surplus matter and feeling that occurs alongside commodified exchanges and seeks a place for it through small gestures of attendant joy.[14]

---

1 Simon, J. () *Neomaterialism.* London: Sternberg Press pp.45.
2 Le Guin, U.K. (2019) *The Carrier Bag Theory of Fiction,* Peru: Ignota Books.
3 Le Guin's theory is based on the studies of anthropologist Elizabeth Fisher who proposes the receptacle as the first human invention, rather than the weapon. Le Guin goes on to explore the effects of Fisher's insight on how human relationships and structures are depicted and how they can be re-imagined, while also re-evaluating the possibilities of historical and contemporary fiction as a vessel.
4 Brown, B. (2001) *Thing Theory. Critical Inquiry,* Vol. 28 (No. 1 Things, Autumn, 2001), pp.1-22. Available at: http://www.jstor.org/stable/1344258 (Accessed 14th April 2024)
5 Barthes, R. (1957) *Mythologies,* trans. Annette Lavers. London: Noonday Press: pp.133.
6 Custom made props used for performances.
7 This led to the need for further packaging, to now protect the packaging that was part of the artwork.
8 Beaver, H. (1981) *Homosexual Signs (In Memory of Roland Barthes),* Critical Inquiry, Vol. 8 (No. 1, Autumn 1981) pp.99-119. Available at: https://www.jstor.org/stable/1343208 (Accessed 14th April 2024)
9 Leung G. (2023) Bosses, Divided Publishing: London, Belgium, pp.33.
10 When I gave the artwork *Protect What Matters* to A.L. via post, he called me to ask if he is meant to open it. There was nothing in the package apart from other packaging forming a layered collage. His question made me wonder when does ownership start: does he own this work if he doesn't open it?
11 Constantinos Kyriakopoulos, informal conversation, Pagrati (August 2020).
12 Mauss, M (1925) *The Gift: The Form and Reason for Exchange in Archaic Societies.* Reprint: 1990. London: Routledge, pp.10.
13 Offer (verb), Cambridge Dictionary. Available at: https://dictionary.cambridge.org/dictionary/english/offer (Accessed 14th April 2024).
14 Tam, E. M L, Conversation with author (02 February 2024).

Our Range:
Lux line
Fine Quality
High Quality
Has a name
High power
Quantity
Elegance
Style
Klass
Classic
Best
Plus
Top
Max
Premium

AAA+
+++
Extra
XTRA
Special
Mega
Ultra
Pro
Smart
Established
Exclusive
Finest
Immortal
New
New & improved
New standards

Super Special
Super Extra
Heavy Duty
Excellent
Expert
Doublex
Multi
Multi-purpose
Multi-function
Adjustable
General
General Purpose
All purpose
Universal
Generic
Essential

The best bargains
Competitive Prices
Get one free
1+1
2 for 1
2 for 2
Multi-Pack
Value Pack
Size
Variety
120 parts
3 rolls
2 pieces
8 labels
x 10
15ps

Friendly Exchanges

Lucy Cowling

Something strange is afoot on the archetypal UK high streets found across towns and city neighbourhoods. Moving with a centrifugal dispersion, away from the uniform big brands and fast fashion, to the less desirable ends of the shopping streets, you can find a retail model that breaks with the late capitalist mould; the charity shop. Some might argue these retailers represent the most distilled form of value extraction; they operate completely on volunteer labour, donated goods, and slashed business rates to generate maximum profit. However, the clothes, knick-knacks, and oddities that trade hands in these spaces point to a more interesting social and economic truth. Crucially, the fact that this profit isn't intended to create wealth, but instead to benefit social good is a key distinction. These systems of circulation retrieve the concept of 'value' from its most narrow capitalist definition, to mean more than mere money. The success of the charity shop shows the possibility of an alternative economy, one that is based on friendly exchanges, gifting, investment of time, and social values. Even though the previous owner will never meet the new owner, there is a relational bond between them, through the object.

The undisputed friend and neighbour of the charity shop are the independently run discount variety retailers. They are these cavernous wonder emporiums where you walk in for a pack of AAA batteries, and end up walking out with a tin can of condensed milk, a hole punch, and some cute patterned socks.[1] Imagine spaces filled floor to ceiling; a true cacophony of things. Some items have bright, eccentric packaging, shouting out for attention. Much of the stock is utilitarian, but there are always sections collecting dust, waiting to be wanted, but who knows what for. The inventory preaches quantity over quality, favouring the slightly naff and factory produced. There is dead stock, and wholesale leftovers that have passed through multiple hands before ending up stacked on these shelves.

Retailers like these are like goldmines for Eleni Papazoglou. For the last couple of years Eleni isn't only frequenting them to buy the items they offer for sale, be it stationary, stickers or office supplies, but also to hunt for discarded boxes or packaging, all of which can become material for artworks. The processes used to acquire these materials include gifting, barter and exchange. It is these social relationships that give true form to the items. They come into being through an embrace of the somewhat unlikely bedfellows of hyper-locality and ubiquity, and the overlooked and the intimate. The unity is formed by knowing how to find and move through very location-specific retail spaces, seeking out the right combination of the generic and desirable. Not dissimilar to what happens within charity shops, the acquisition processes cut through the usual systems of circulation and capital gain. Crucially, changing the use and status of these objects has a profound effect on their 'thingness'; their ability to communicate and synthesise.[2]

The hyper-local and the ubiquitous

Eleni Papazoglou is based between Athens and South London. These two localities have a far reaching influence on the outcomes of Eleni's works. The presence of Peckham Rye Lane, Vauxhall Market and Deptford High Street in London and Evripidou and Athinas Street in central Athens can be viscerally felt, at times by being the source of small material elements, but mainly by serving as sites of research for concepts pertaining to retail display, packaging, and object circulation.

For example, Evripidou Street is lined with various specialist wholesalers, convenience stores, and packaging and catering suppliers. One such shop sells laminated menus, the type where each dish is represented by a photographed plate of food. The menu has intentional blank spaces, so that each restaurant using it can add their own prices. A completely mass-produced item, shipped into Athens, sold in a retailer selling to other businesses, made to be tailored to the economic demands of a beach-front strip somewhere many hundreds of kilometres away. For this item to come into being, it will somehow have implicated a food stylist, photographer, perhaps a graphic designer. For it to exist as a commodity, the subjectivities of those who delivered and sold it can be added to this list, as well as a restaurateur, customer, and chef — who presumably now has to stand in a kitchen trying to mimic the dish in the original image. It is a perfect conflation of how the needs of a particular community interact with general, globalised, systems of exchange. It shows that the commodity's material is constituted by our social relations."[3] The hyper-local and the global are too often pitched as a dichotomy, whereas more often goods exist within a third possibility; where local variation flavours and ultimately reforms the factory mould.

Deptford High Street and Rye Lane in the south east pocket of the city are similarly shaped by very specific socio-economic factors. They are

---

1   I'm imagining my local one-stop-shop, Khan's Bargains in Peckham, South London. A firm favourite, they sum this idea up in their Google Maps business description perfectly: "WE ARE SELLING EVERYTHING (EXCEPT ALCOHOL AND FRESH MEAT.) WE SALE FRESH FRUIT AND VEG DAIRY PRODUCTS BEANS AND RICE AND FLOUR SEASONING AND CANNED FOOD TOILETRIES COSMETICS STATIONERY BEDDING KITCHENWARE AND GARDEN PRODUCTS ELICTRIC AND D I Y AND LUGGAGE AND MOBILE ACCESSORIES" [sic]
2   Heidegger, M. (1968) *What is a Thing?*. Chicago: Gateway Books, pp. 11.
3   Hirsh, A. (2011) *Intangible Economies*. Available at: https://fillip.ca/content/intangible-economies (accessed 14 February 2024).

filled with life, busy with consumers seeking out the West African or Vietnamese supermarkets, frequenting shops with staple household goods, market traders selling second hand items and fruit and vegetables by the bowl. The stories of these streets are highly localised, unique to each place, but formed through long and rich histories of human migration, geo-politics and global commodity circulation. What these two shopping streets have in common is that they are dominated by independent businesses rather than chains, which is often key, both to build familiarity and trust with those working in the shops, and to finding idiosyncratic and surprising inventories.

The items that make their way from these spaces to Eleni's studio are ubiquitous; they're often standardised, manufactured in bulk. What makes them specific are the traces of places and relationships that exist within the items. What makes them more interesting are the additional social bonds that brought these objects out of their intended cycle of circulation and into the artist's studio.

The overlooked and the intimate

Not far from the packaging supply shop, on Athinas Street — a busy thoroughfare in central Athens — there is a shop that sells everything that has to do with doors but isn't a door; handles, knobs, hinges, locks and the like. This was the source of a particularly seductive piece of packaging. Canary yellow, with the words 'AKA' repeatedly plastered diagonally across it in a deep and vivid blue, something about the design of this empty door handle board box, elicited a hoarder's response, meaning it made its way back to London and into the studio.

Desire is a strong economic driver.[4] It signifies by way of circulation and it finds its expression through the human interactions it engenders. What does it mean when the thing that is desired is an empty box? Usually overlooked; it is the wrapper to be discarded, made as a container for, or a means to. Now it is a thing in its own right. When pieces are incorporated into artworks, these otherwise discarded materials become intimately acquainted with each other, through being fused together, collaged, laser cut and carefully layered.

There is also another form of intimacy at play in the material gathering and art making processes. A fair amount of the packaging and stationery items are gifts from friends.[5] Whether stumbled upon in an off licence, given as a surprise, or instructed to seek out and bring back from far-away travels, these items carry the attention and love of another person within them. In exchange, Eleni has made particular pieces with someone specific in mind. In fact, after years of gathering packaging and paraphernalia with no particular purpose, the collected boxes and stickers first took on new forms collaged onto postcards, which were sent out as individual gifts to friends.[6] That project was the seed for this current body of work. Whilst invisible to most viewers, these relationships leave their traces on the outcomes; the people and the places are intrinsically enmeshed with the artworks.

When the thing calls out

It was Martin Heidegger's belief that an object becomes a thing once it can no longer serve its primary purpose.[7] This 'productive estrangement' is a cornerstone of thing theory, a branch of cultural analysis that sprung up around the turn of the millennium to explore the dynamics between inanimate objects and human subjects, within the structures of commodity capitalism.[8] The premise is that people become most aware of an object's agency when they are taken out of the usual context, when the object starts to break, or when it is otherwise 'misused'. Out of all the social relationships that shape the object, it is those who "clean, dismantle and scavenge" for it who most make it a thing.[9] Artists who work with objects and materials fabricated outside of the studio play this role well. Contemporary art practice makes the wider world appear before the viewer. It is a great vehicle for what Heidegger called "the thingness of the thing"[10]; essentially what is being communicated beyond physical appearance and utility, or the "essence that allows the object to stand on its own".[11]

It takes practice and an open-minded approach to tune in to this form of communication. Walter Benjamin was concerned with what things might be trying to say to us, or were conversing about with each other, in his text *On Language as Such and on the Language of Man*. For him, the language of things is full of potential, as it has the possibility to actively transform material, social, and historical relations.[12] In his definition, 'language' constitutes more than what is spoken within a particular

---

4   Hirsh, A. (2011) *Intangible Economies: Preface*. Available at: https://fillip.ca/content/intangible-economies-preface (accessed 15 February 2024).
5   Papazoglou E., interview with author (12 February 2024).
6   Papazoglou E., interview with author (12 February 2024).
7   Wasserman, S. (2020) *Thing Theory*. Oxford Bibliographies of Literary and Critical Theory. Available at: https://www.oxfordbibliographies.com/display/document/obo-9780190221911/obo-9780190221911-0097.xml (accessed 14 February 2024).
8   ibid.
9   Simon, J. (2013), *Neomaterialism*. London: Sternberg Press, pp. 79 — 104.
10 Heidegger, M. (1968) *What is a Thing?*. Chicago: Gateway Books, pp. 32.
11 Gyorody, A. and Johnson, E. (2019) *The Thingness of Things: Portraits of Objects*. Available at: https://amam.oberlin.edu/exhibitions-events/exhibitions/2019/02/05/the-thingness-of-things-portraits-of-objects (accessed 15 February 2024).
12 Steyerl, H. (2006) *The Language of Things*. Available at: https://transversal.at/transversal/0606/steyerl/ (accessed 18 February 2024).

geographic boundary, he also includes the language of art, law and technology. Language then is not definite by national borders, but by a common practice. "According to Benjamin", Hito Steyerl sums up, "this language of things is mute, it is magical and its medium is material community".[13] Whilst "mute", things are therefore not speechless, and translation occurs *within* these expanded fields of language as well as between.[14] Steyerl continues, "That humans decided to rule over things and to disregard their message led to the disaster at Babylon. To start listening to them again would be the first step towards a coming common language, which is not rooted in the hypocrite presumption of a unity of humankind, but in a much more general material community."[15] Acts of translation, to be understood here as seeking out shared community through material culture, thereby amplifies the ways that things can change how we relate to the wider world.

Learning the local language

Though, "of course," Maggie Nelson wrote in *The Art of Cruelty*, "not all 'thingness' is created equal, and one has to live enough of one's life *not* as a thing to know the difference".[16] Nelson is talking about negative affect produced through objectification. Read within the context of Heideggers' distinction between objects and things, and specifically how this changes the subject-object relationship between people and material, the reverse holds more sway; 'one has to live enough of one's life as a thing to know the difference'. That is to say, those who live their lives outside of the normative frameworks, or those who don't engage much with the attention economy and commodity culture, are the most attune to understanding the language of things.

Along with the language of *things*, there is another language that must be mastered to be successful in the quest to obtain material – be it stock or cast-away packaging – through barter, donation or exchange; that of retail spaces. These shops are coded spaces. There is constant translation taking place. Pitching requests at the right tone, appeasing, coming across with genuine and serious intent, whilst making what could well be perceived as an odd request requires a careful navigation of each vernacular. The language needs to be tweaked for each site, or even each interpersonal interaction.

A pursuit to acquire desired material is most likely to work out if the relational bonds, trust built up over time or through friendship, are intrinsically linked to shared knowledge. Convivial exchanges, albeit brief, act like social glue.[17] In the tradition of Benjamin and Steyerl, these interactions are founded in a particular form of intimacy, where the sense of place or common origin isn't tied to nationhood but to a very particular practice. It is this transcendence of nationalist or even cultural identity that can knit together the generic mass-produced objects with their innate 'thingness', formed by the context in which they've been sourced or scavenged.

Part and parcel

"Love don't cost a thing", J-Lo sang back in the early 2000s.[18] Given that emotions, in particular desire, are catalysts for social transactions and thereby big drivers of value, this statement takes on a fair bit of artistic licence. It is true that value generation doesn't necessarily denote monetary gain, as "love is immaterial capital in the absolute, in a sphere of value relations where capital and labour are no longer the main operators or arbiters of value".[19] In other words, our social relations help to give form to the economy, which in turn spurs on further behaviours.

Material culture and social relationships are inextricably entwined. As such, the items collected by Eleni are shaped by human connection, donation, and location. Commenting on the importance of this, Heidegger noted in *What is a Thing?* that, "place and time make even absolutely identical things [. . .] different ones."[20] What might therefore seem like a ubiquitous bit of material carries with it the subjectivities of all those that handled it, intimately shaped by hyper-local conditions. The yellow 'AKA' box for example, contains all the social interactions and economic transactions that meant it ended up in that particular door knob shop in central Athens, rather than a hardware supplier in London. Ultimately, material is "love and time".[21] It is through reciprocal exchange of both material goods and immaterial values that social solidarity can be built.[22] This is a core argument in *The Gift,* an essay from 1925 by Marcel Mauss, which is a sociological

---

13 ibid.
14 Cunningham, D. (2016) *If Things Could Speak*. Available at: https://www.fotomuseum.ch/en/2016/06/13/if-things-could-speak/ (accessed 18 February 2024).
15 Steyerl, H. (2006) *The Language of Things*. Available at: https://transversal.at/transversal/0606/steyerl/ (accessed 18 February 2024).
16 In her case she is explaining why the "meat-making" of gale male porn "doesn't produce the same species of anxiety" as straight porn, see Nelson, M. (2011) *The Art of Cruelty: A Reckoning*. New York City: W. W. Norton & Co., pp. 183.
17 Laing, O. (2016) *The Lonely City*, Edinburgh: Canongate Books, pp. 119.
18 Lopez, J. (2001) *Love Don't Cost a Thing*. Prod.: Wake, R., Jones, R., and Rooney, C. Los Angeles: Epic Records.
19 Wood, B. K. (2014) *Is it Love?* E-flux journal issue #53. Available at: https://www.e-flux.com/journal/53/59897/is-it-love/ (accessed 1 March 2024).
20 Heidegger, M. (1968) *What is a Thing?*. Chicago: Gateway Books, pp. 17.
21 White, I (2011) *What is Material?* Cited in Jones, E. (2019) *A Queer Politics of Entanglement: Alex Baczynski-Jenkins in conversation with Eliel Jones*. Mousse Magazine. Available at https://www.moussemagazine.it/magazine/alex-baczynski-jenkins-eliel-jones-2019/ (accessed 1 March 2024).
22 Mauss, M (1925) *The Gift: The Form and Reason for Exchange in Archaic Societies*. Reprint: 1990. London: Routledge, pp. 4.

study of societies that don't use money or "forms of contract and sale that may be said to be modern (Semitic, Hellenic, Hellenistic, and Roman)".[23] Mauss asserts that the gift economy is the base of all systems of exchange and thereby both underpins and undermines our current system of capitalism.

    The elements that constitute the various strategies to acquire material are investing into a greater understanding of common practice and local knowledge — which is to say, listening to the language of things — as well as building on friendships and acts of reciprocity. At times this happens very directly; there is a dealer of motorcycle decal stickers in Psyri, one of Athens' oldest neighbourhoods, who allows Eleni to obtain odd pairs of the best sets in exchange for conversations about his landscape paintings, made in situ whilst on motorbike road trips.[24] Eleni's browsing of stickers obviously didn't follow the patterns of the usual biker custom. At first this aroused some vague suspicion, which was quickly overtaken by curiosity and conversation. Upon establishing that they were being acquired as potential art materials, a common denominator was established as the dealer revealed themselves to be a keen painter, and so the relationship could grow. Now upon most returns to Athens there is a moment of reciprocity about recently made works, along with stories of the trips taken and the best roadside painting spots. This type of exchange of goods, founded in friendly social interactions, can be read as a blueprint; a rally call to listen not only to the inanimate things around us, but also to tune in to each other, to be attentive to the long string of small social interactions that resulted in an object being made, moved, or otherwise meddled with.

---

23 ibid.
24 Papazoglou E., interview with author (12 February 2024).

Products & Services

Products & Services

ITEM CODE	SIZE	BRAND	ITEM	USE / APPLICATION
	SCALE	SOURCE	NOTES	

New Old Stock (NOS)

ITEM CODE	SIZE	BRAND	ITEM	USE / APPLICATION
	SCALE	SOURCE	NOTES	

Catering	CA
Electronics	EL
Haberdashery	HB
Homeware	HW
Motor Accessories	MA
Outdoor & Garden	OG
Shop Accessories	SA
Stationery	ST
Wholesale	WS

ITEM CODE	SIZE	BRAND	ITEM	USE / APPLICATION
	SCALE	SOURCE	NOTES	

**OG
NA
867
250180**

**OG
MJ
926
25090**

**MA
UF
7990
4060B**

OG-NA-867-250180	250x180mm	N/A	Product Label	Tour Mat
	25%	N/A	Donated by Greg & Clara	
OG-MJ-926-25090	250x90 mm	Major Value	Packaging	Garden pruning shears
	25%	55 Nigel Road, SET Social	Discarded	
MA-UF-7990-4060B	40x60 mm	Ultra Firenze	Sticker	Promotional
	50%	Dianele Gianetti	Gifted	

ITEM CODE	SIZE	BRAND	ITEM	USE / APPLICATION
	SCALE	SOURCE	NOTES	

**HD
BA
885
5035D**

**SA
CA
903
8555**

**HB
WH
958
240175A**

**ST
NA
892
5035R**

HD-BA-885-5035D	50x35mm	Basic	N/A	N/A
	25%	HSDS Studio	Gifted	
SA-CA-903-8555	85x55mm	N/A	Price tag	Two-sided price display [side 1/2]
	25%	Christodoulakis, H., - Z. Christodoulaki O.E.		
ST-NA-892-5035R	50x35mm	N/A	Sticker	Greek alphabet
	50%	N/A	N/A	
HB-WH-958-240175A	240x175mm	The Woman and the Home [magazine]	Embroidery Pattern [folded]	Decorating fabric
	25%	Stathmos Old Books Store	N/A	

ITEM CODE	SIZE	BRAND	ITEM	USE / APPLICATION
	SCALE	SOURCE	NOTES	

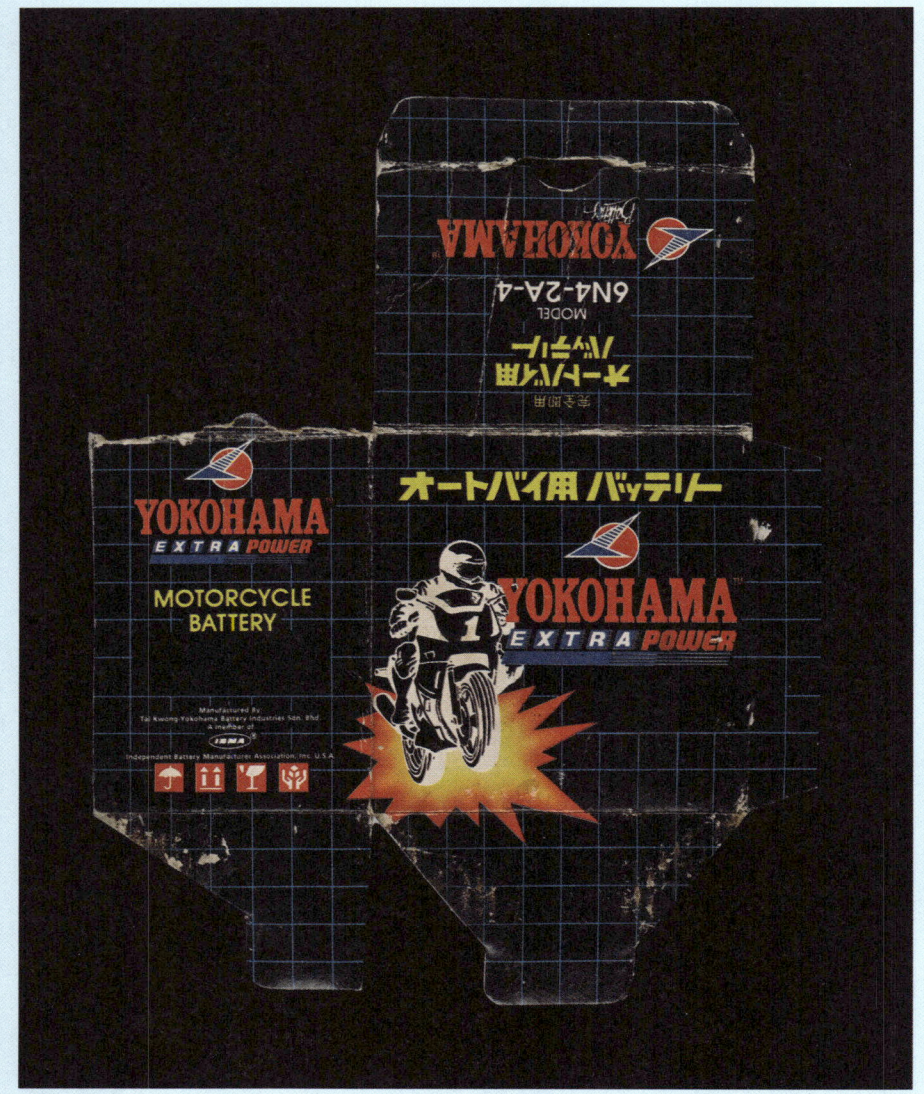

MA
YO
863
250195

HD
SU
8006
240180B

HD
NA
8004
38035A

MA-YO-863-250195	250x195mm	YOKOHAMA	Box	Packaging for motorbike battery
	25%	Epidavros, GR	Donated by Lefki Varangi	
HD-SU-8006-240180B	240x180mm	Supreme	Packaging	Flooring Trims
	25%	55 Nigel Road, SET Social	Discarded	
HD-NA-8004-38035A	380x35mm	N/A	Packaging	Mounting tape
	50%	55 Nigel Road, SET Social	Discarded	

ITEM CODE	SIZE	BRAND	ITEM	USE / APPLICATION
	SCALE	SOURCE	NOTES	

ST NA 883 4040

ST NA 895 15090

ST BL 896 13090

MA AR 7990 3560D

ST-BL-896-13090	130x90mm	Blick	Packaging	Office stickers
	50%	Bright Printers & Stationers	Discarded	
ST-NA-883-4040	40x40mm	N/A	Sticker	Metallic prize
	25%	Bright Printers & Stationers	N/A	
ST-NA-895-15090	150x90mm	Super Initial HK	Sticker in package	Vinyl sticker
	25%	Lucas Dupuy	Gifted	
MA-AR-7990-3560D	35x60mm	Arrow	Sticker	Promotional
	50%	Dianele Gianetti	Gifted	

ITEM CODE	SIZE	BRAND	ITEM	USE / APPLICATION
	SCALE	SOURCE	NOTES	
HW-AK-866-350220	350x220mm	AKA	Box lid	Packaging for door handles
	25%	Bardis	Donated after attempt of theft	
EL-TE-893-12030	120x30mm	T&E	Packaging	Alkaline battery set 1.55v
	200%	Galatsi Flea Market	N/A	
HD-NA-940-145124	145x124mm	Fischer	Paper bag [part of]	Hardware store
	100%	Rokkas Angeliki	Discarded	

ITEM CODE	SIZE	BRAND	ITEM	USE / APPLICATION
	SCALE	SOURCE	NOTES	

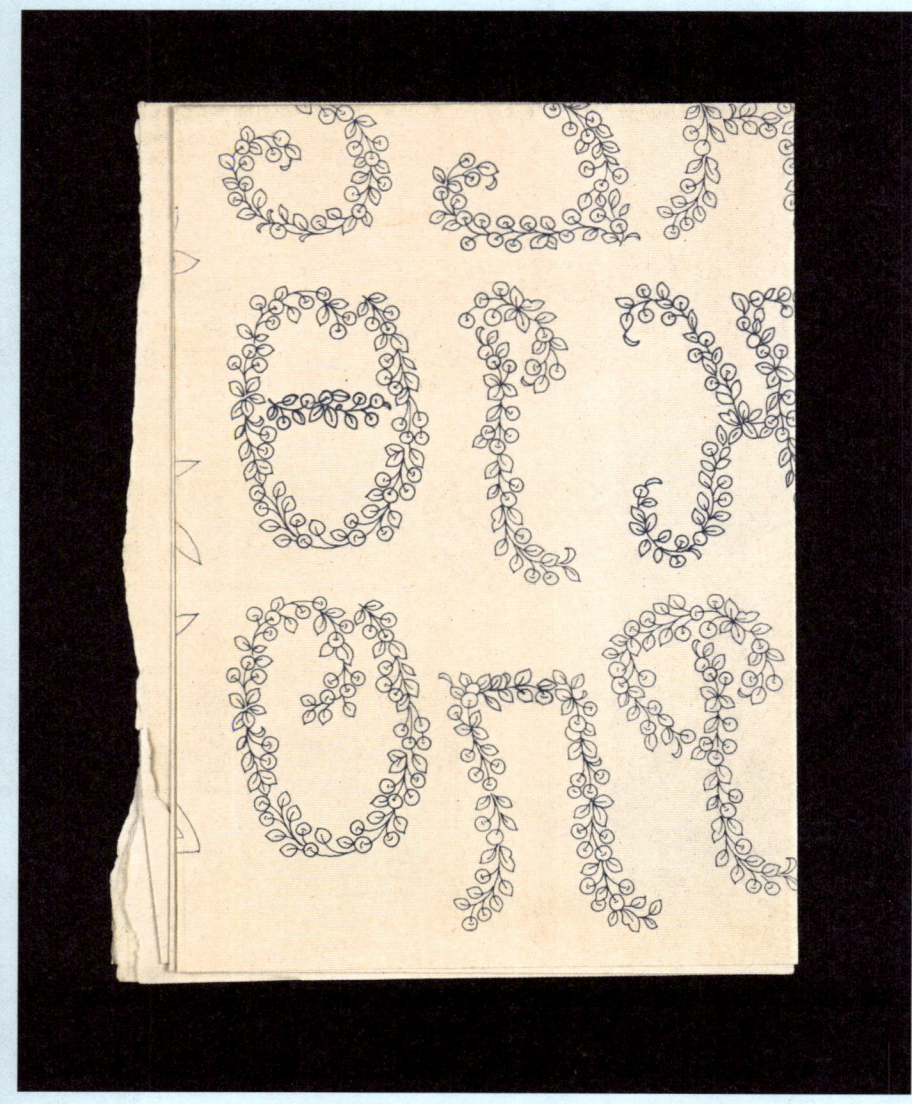

**HB
PR
946
240175B**

**ST
NA
002A
13080**

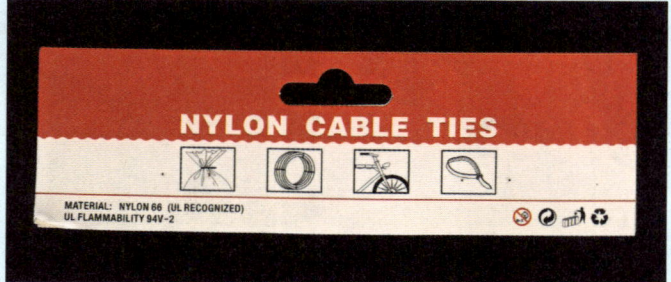

**HD
NA
8806
80435F**

HB-PR-946-240175B	240x175mm	Practice Magazine	Embroidery pattern	Decorating fabric
	25%	Kougeas Used Books	N/A	
ST-NA-002A-13080	130x80mm	N/A	Sticker Set	Numbered labels
	25%	N/A	N/A	
HD-NA-8806-80435F	80x435mm	N/A	Packaging	Nylon cable ties
	25%	N/A	Discarded	

ITEM CODE	SIZE	BRAND	ITEM	USE / APPLICATION
	SCALE	SOURCE	NOTES	

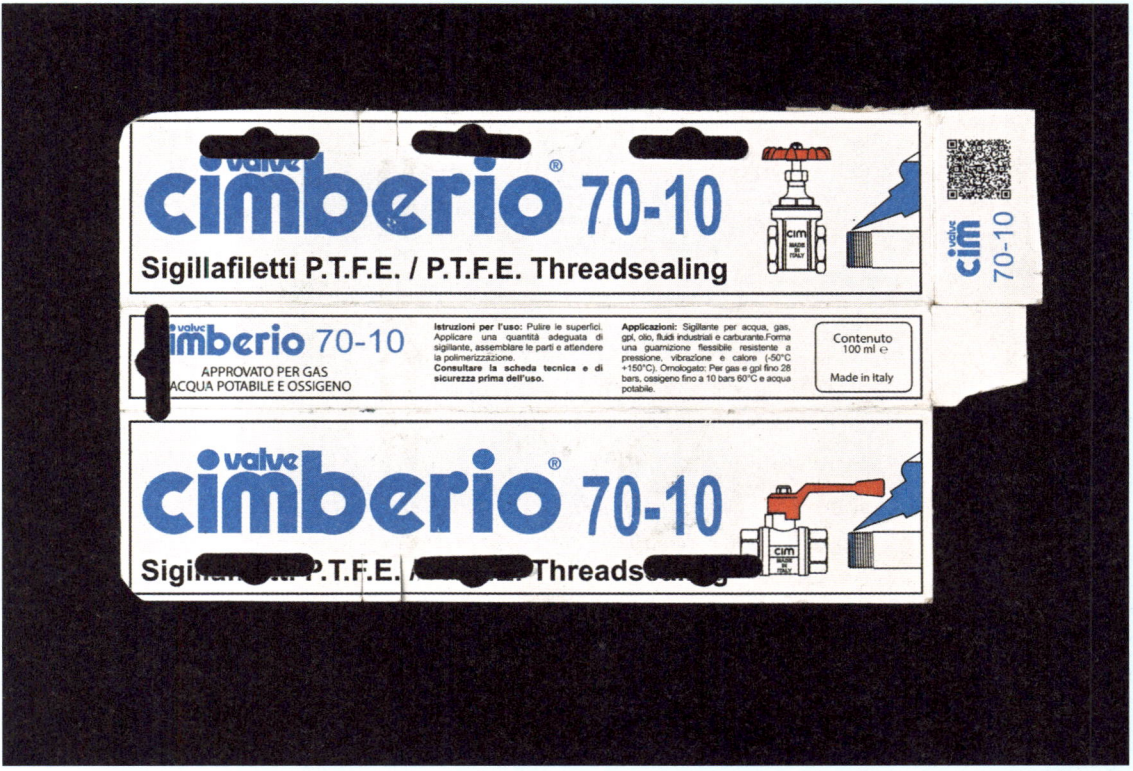

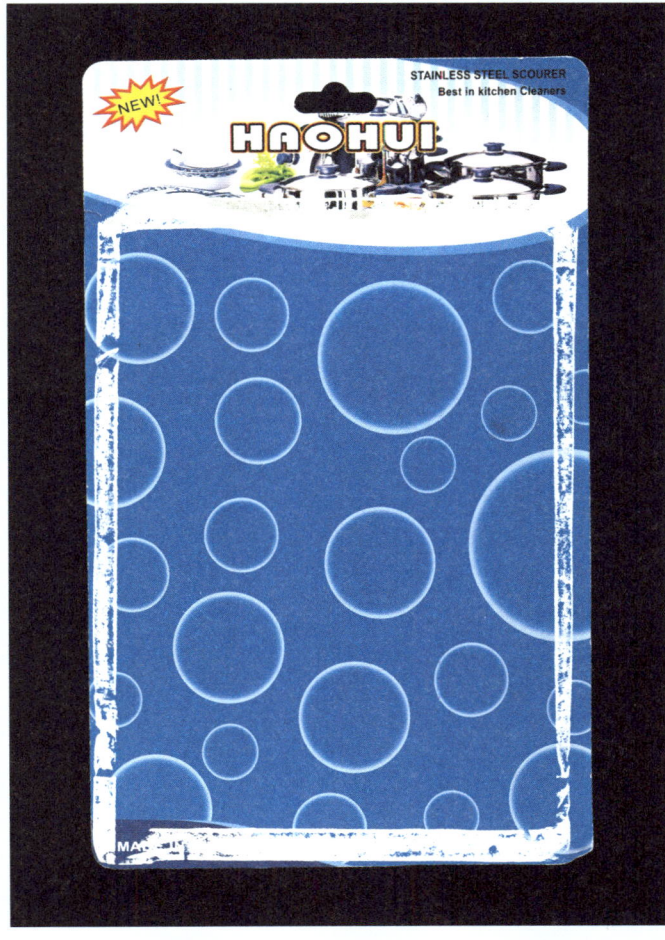

HD CI 864 240138

HW HA 965 260163

ST NA 002C 13080

HD-CI-864-240138	240x138mm	Cimberio	Box	P.T.F.E. Threadsealing
	25%	Exarchia Flea Market	Discarded	
HW-HA-965-260163	260x163mm	HAOHUI	Packaging backing	Stainless steel scourers
	25%	Exarchia Flea Market	Found on the street	
ST-NA-002C-13080	130x80mm	N/A	Sticker Set	Postal
	25%	N/A	N/A	

ITEM CODE	SIZE	BRAND	ITEM	USE / APPLICATION
	SCALE	SOURCE	NOTES	

HD NH 7990 5030E

HW EN 924 148105

SA SL 925 195125

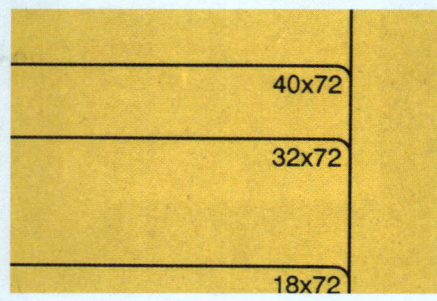

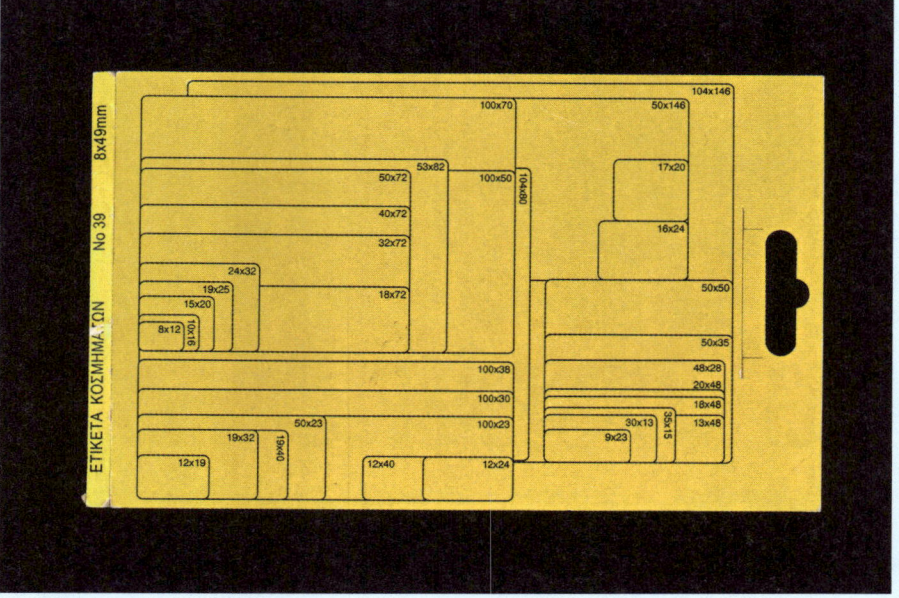

HW-EN-924-148105	148x105mm	ENERGY	Product Label	Element from car sponge wrapping
	50%	N/A	European Product	
HD-NH-7990-5030E	50x30mm	New Holland	Packaging	N/A
	50%	N/A	Discarded	
SA-SL-925-195125	195x125mm	Stef-Labels	Packaging [back of]	Wholesale package of jewellery labels
	25%	Stoa Kairi	Made in Hellas	

ITEM CODE	SIZE	BRAND	ITEM	USE / APPLICATION
	SCALE	SOURCE	NOTES	
MA-NA-987-1501130	150x1130mm	N/A	Decal	Motorbike
	50%	Tourtoglou Prodromos	N/A	
MA-HO-977-70560K	70x560mm	Honda	Decal	Astrea Supra
	50%	Tourtoglou Prodromos	N/A	
MA-YA-981-105230	105x230mm	N/A	Decal	Yamaha XT
	100%	Tourtoglou Prodromos	N/A	

ITEM CODE	SIZE	BRAND	ITEM	USE / APPLICATION
	SCALE	SOURCE	NOTES	

ST
NA
895
15090B

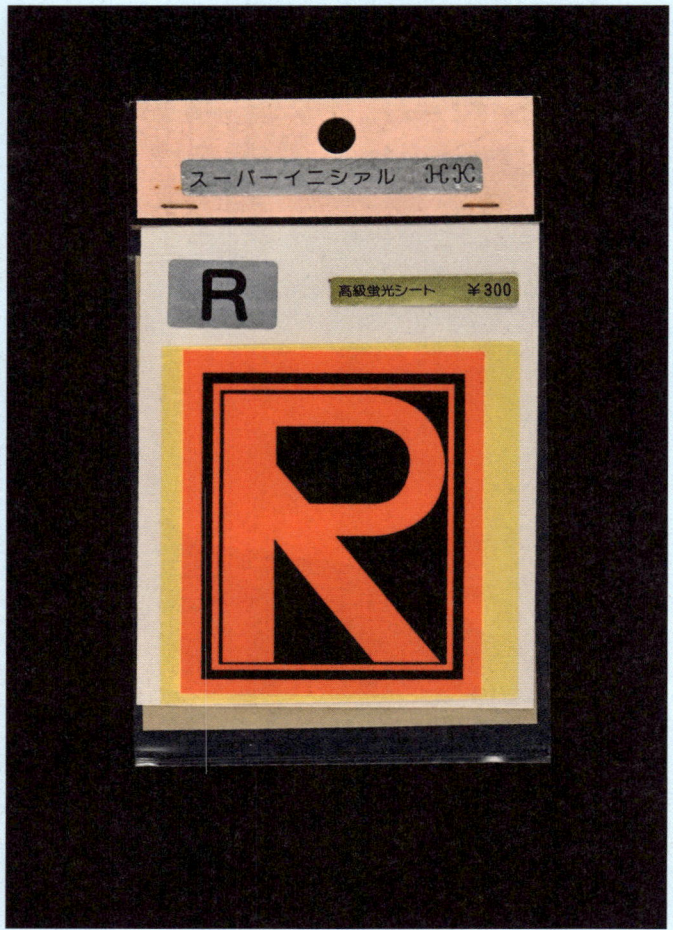

HD
NA
901
180100

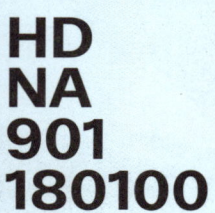 

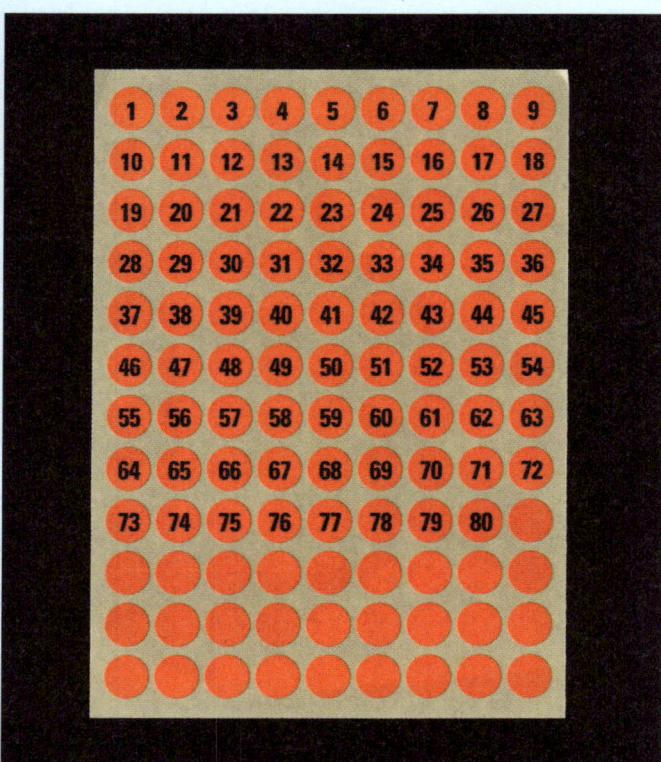

ST
NA
8006
350240E

ST-NA-895-15090B	150x90mm	Super Initial HK	Sticker in package	Vinyl sticker
	25%	Lucas Dupuy	Gifted	
HD-NA-901-180100	180x100mm	N/A	Box	2 in 1 Scale and Tape Measure
	25%	Kiosk	Discarded	
ST-NA-8006-350240E	350x240mm	N/A	Sticker Set	Color dots [orange]
	50%	Kim's Newsagent	N/A	

ITEM CODE	SIZE	BRAND	ITEM	USE / APPLICATION
	SCALE	SOURCE	NOTES	

OG HE 891 5580

SA WS 923 26570B

HW HE 011 1401035

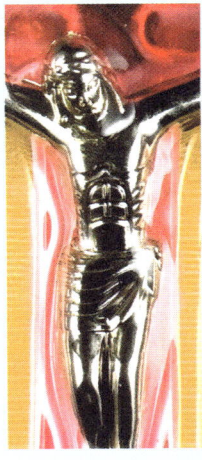

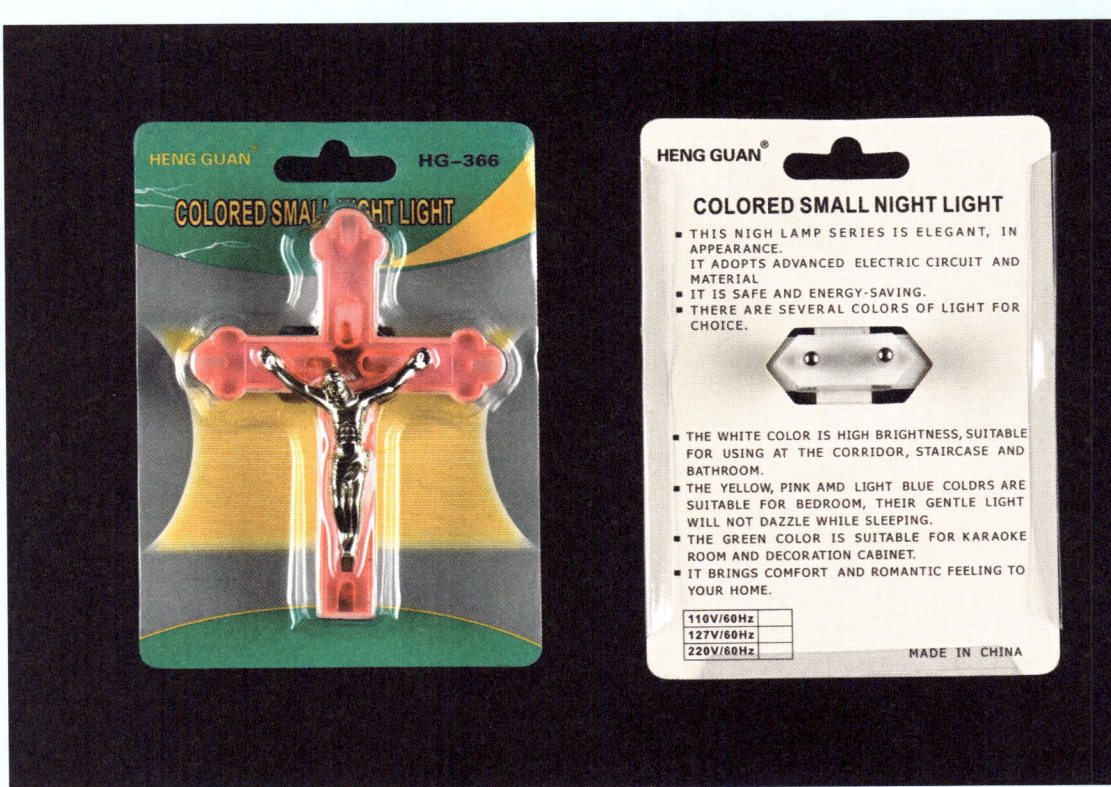

SA-WS-923-26570B	265x70mm	N/A	Plastic Bag [part of]	Wholesale product for tourist shops
	25%	N/A	Acquired while shopping	
HW-HE-011-1401035	140x103x58mm	HENG-GUAN	Packaging	Small night light
	25%	Kypseli Flea Market	Front and back	
OG-HE-891-5580	55x80mm	Henbrandt Ltd	Packaging	Fun Snaps
	25%	Khan's Bargains	Not for sale to persons under 16	

ITEM CODE	SIZE	BRAND	ITEM	USE / APPLICATION
	SCALE	SOURCE	NOTES	

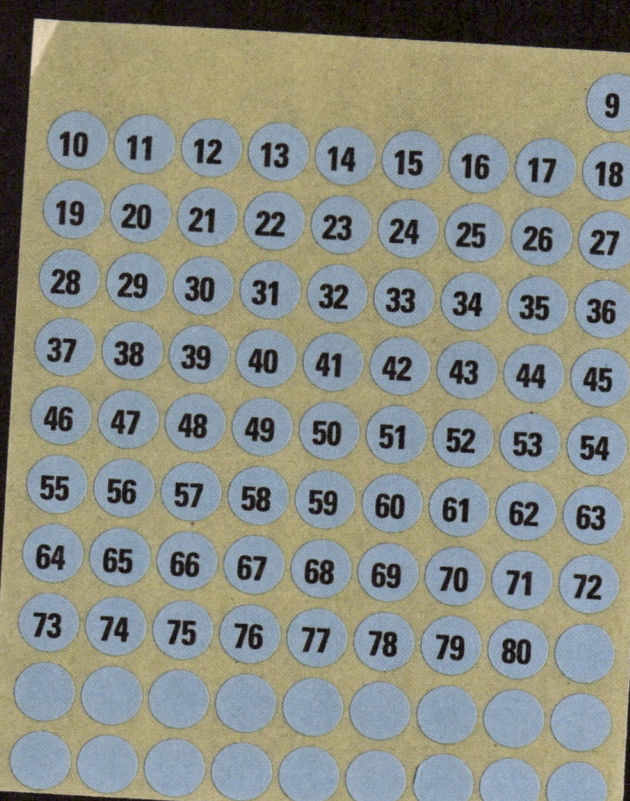

ST-HE-8004-260240A

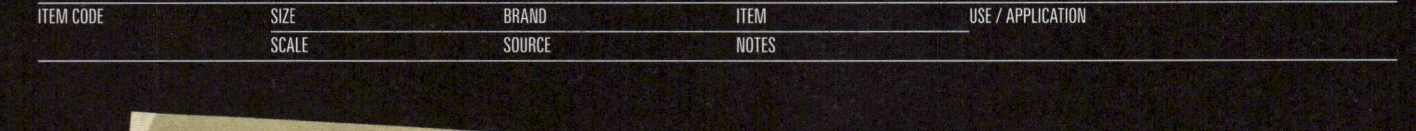

ST-NA-002B-10770

SA-BL-8004-13078

SA-SL-002D-130107

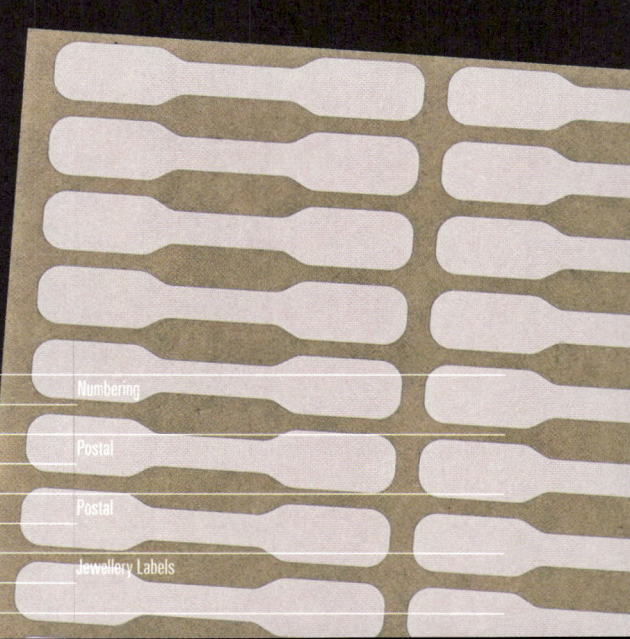

ST-HE-8004-10584A	105x84mm	Vario Hermia	Sticker Set	Numbering
	100%	VIVLIOCHARTIKI Ltd.	N/A	
ST-NA-002B-10770	107x70mm	N/A	Sticker Set	Postal
	100%	N/A	Final request	
SA-BL-8004-13078	130x78mm	Blick	Sticker Set	Postal
	100%	Lasheen The Stationer	N/A	
SA-SL-002D-130107	130x107mm	Stef-Labels	Price Tags	Jewellery Labels
	100%	Stoa Kairi	Made in Hellas	

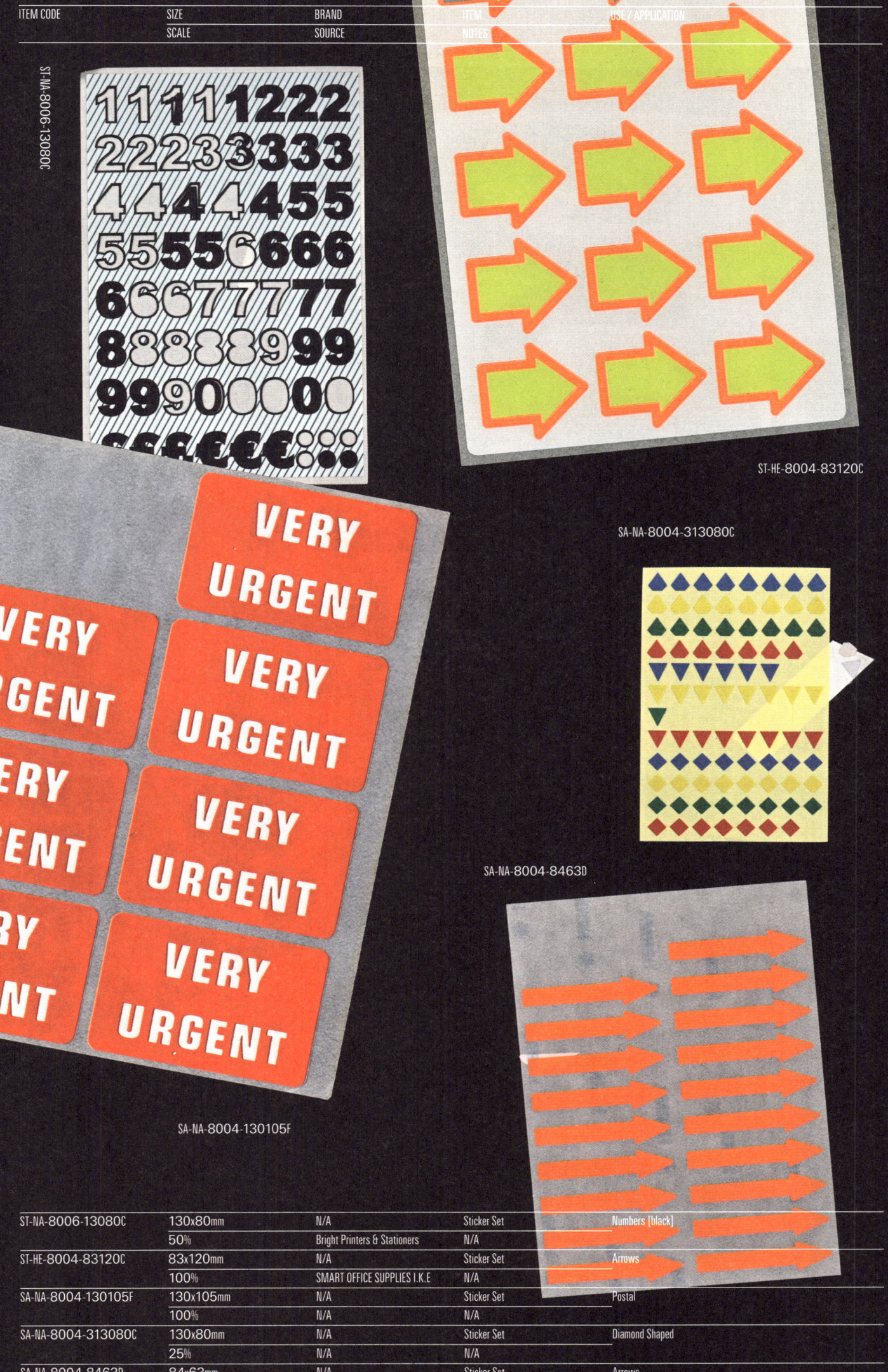

ITEM CODE	SIZE	BRAND	ITEM	USE / APPLICATION
	SCALE	SOURCE	NOTES	
ST-NA-8006-13080C	130x80mm	N/A	Sticker Set	Numbers (black)
	50%	Bright Printers & Stationers	N/A	
ST-HE-8004-83120C	83x120mm	N/A	Sticker Set	Arrows
	100%	SMART OFFICE SUPPLIES I.K.E	N/A	
SA-NA-8004-130105F	130x105mm	N/A	Sticker Set	Postal
	100%	N/A	N/A	
SA-NA-8004-313080C	130x80mm	N/A	Sticker Set	Diamond Shaped
	25%	N/A	N/A	
SA-NA-8004-8463D	84x63mm	N/A	Sticker Set	Arrows
	50%	N/A	N/A	

ITEM CODE	SIZE	BRAND	ITEM	USE / APPLICATION
	SCALE	SOURCE	NOTES	

ST
BI
8006
350240A

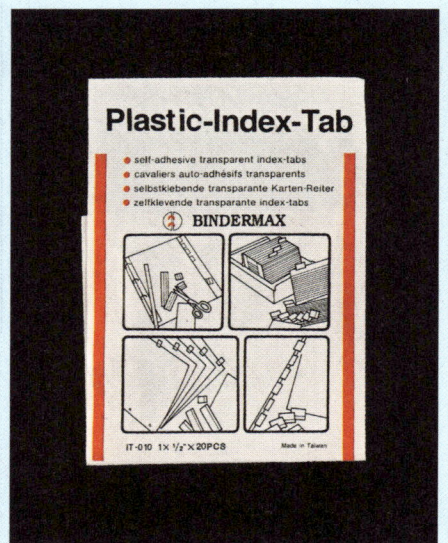

MA
NA
974
145158

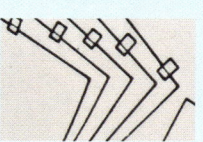

ST
LI
859
250175

ITEM CODE	SIZE	BRAND	ITEM	USE / APPLICATION
MA-NA-974-145158	145x158mm	N/A	Decal	Number for motorbike
	25%	Tourtoglou Prodromos	N/A	
ST-BI-8006-350240A	350x240mm	Bindermax	Packaging	Plastic index tabs
	25%	Egglezos Vafeiadakis	Sourced at Legal Stationery Shop	
ST-LI-859-250175	250x175mm	Lion Triangles	Triangular paper envelope	Set square set
	75%	N/A	N/A	

ITEM CODE	SIZE	BRAND	ITEM	USE / APPLICATION
	SCALE	SOURCE	NOTES	
EL-SD-868-357237	357x237mm	SDNMY	Box	High power battery
	25%	Recycling bin, Fuda Trading Company	N/A	

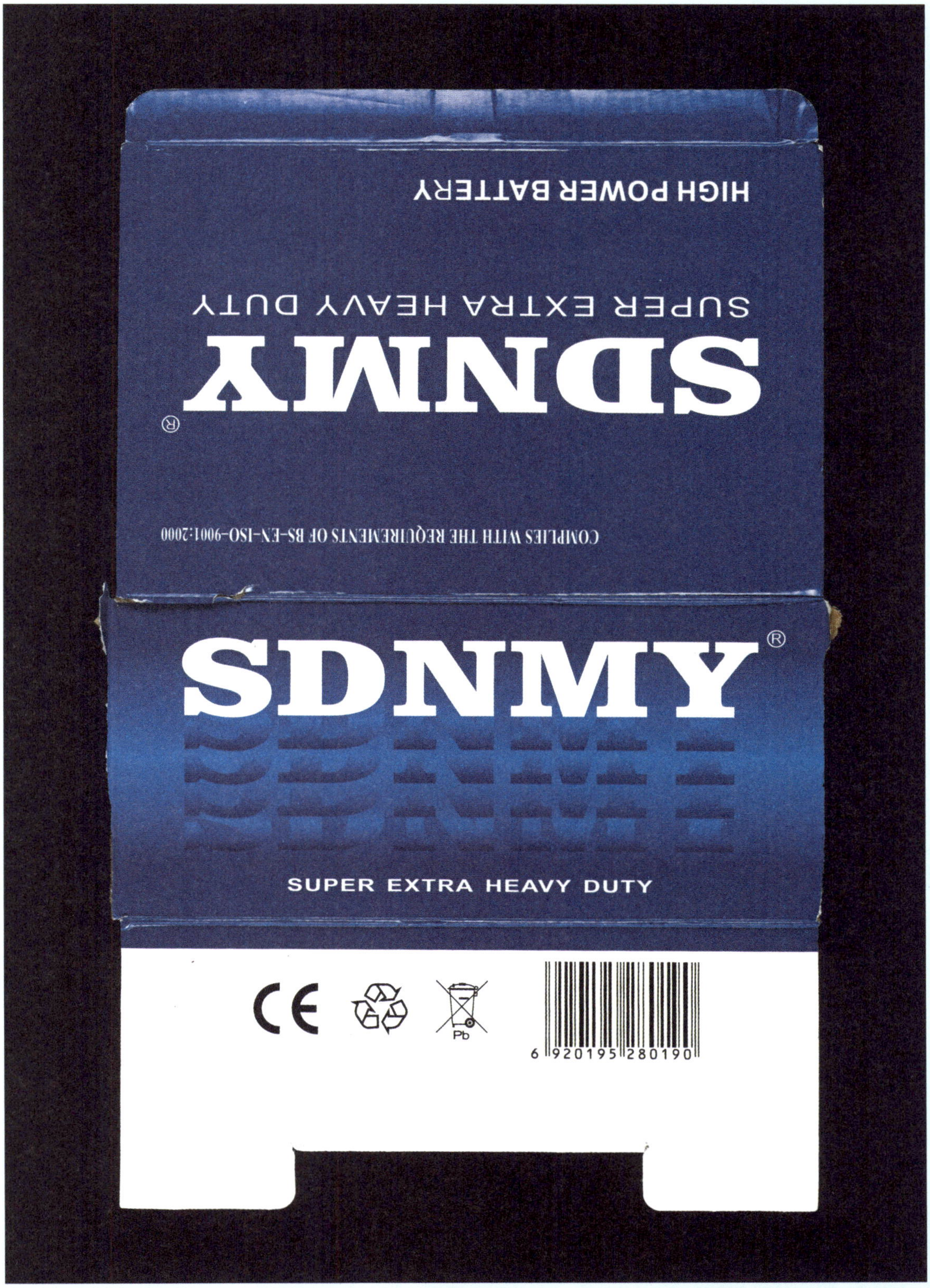

EL
SD
868
357237

ITEM CODE	SIZE	BRAND	ITEM	USE / APPLICATION
	SCALE	SOURCE	NOTES	

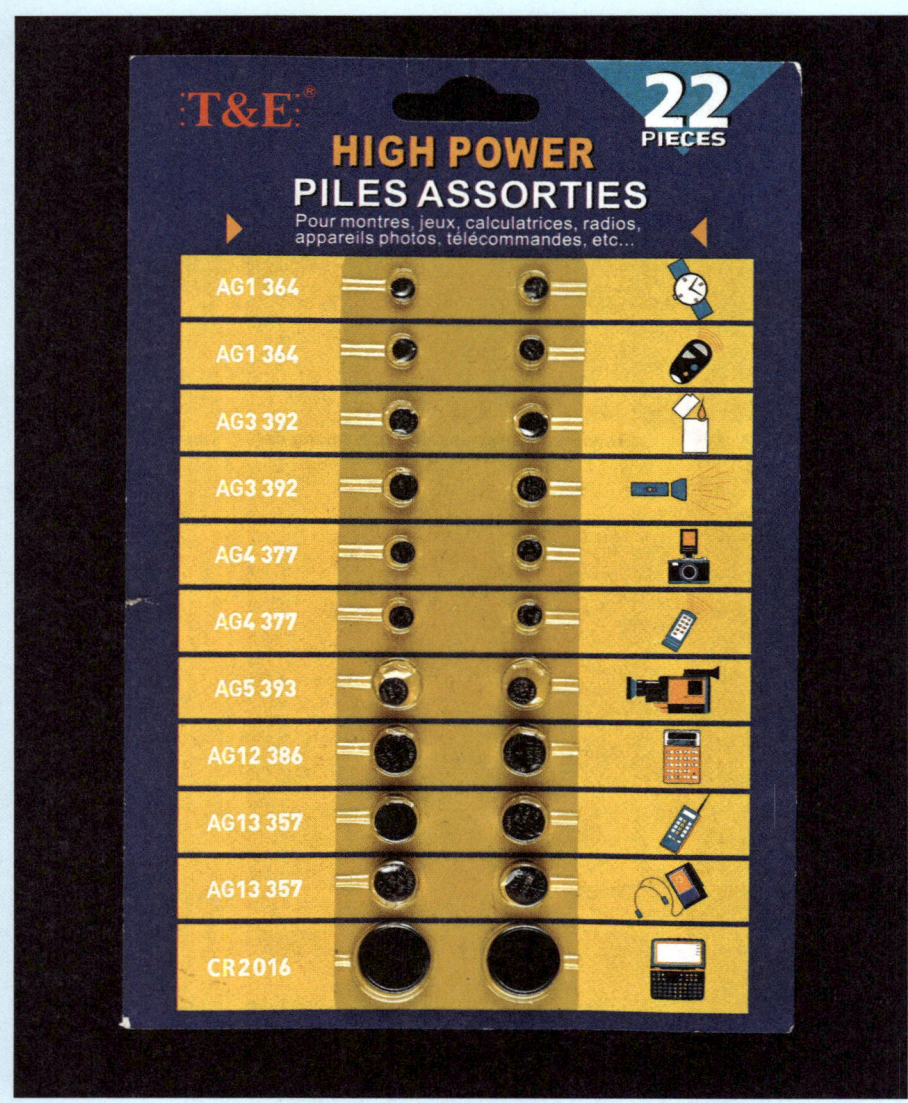

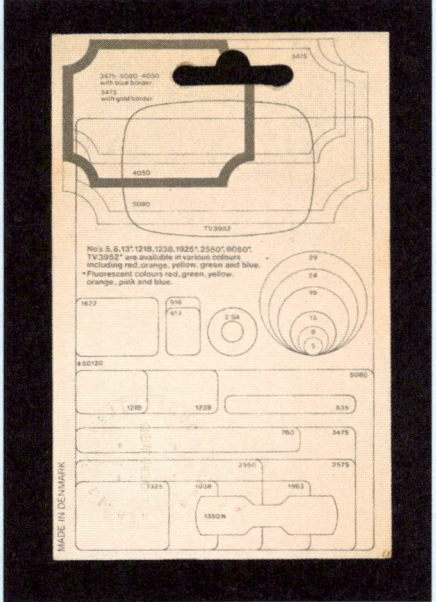

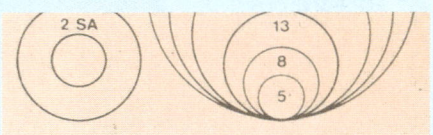

ST BL 897 13090

HW TO 7914 260110

EL TE 861 265180

MA NA 895 100120

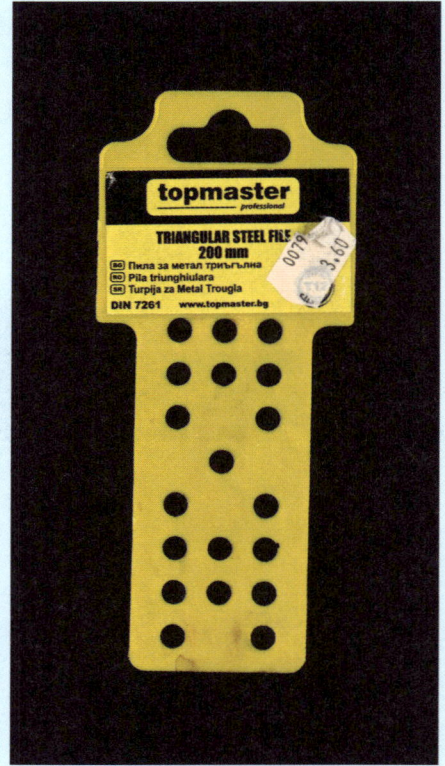

EL-TE-861-265180	265x180mm	T&E	Packaging	Battery pack [22 pieces]
	50%	Kypseli Flea Market	N/A	
ST-BL-897-13090	130x90mm	N/A	Packaging	Labels
	25%	Bright Printers & Stationers	Made in Denmark	
HW-T0-7914-260110	260x110mm	Topmaster	Packaging	Triangular steel file
	25%	N/A	N/A	

ITEM CODE	SIZE	BRAND	ITEM	USE / APPLICATION
	SCALE	SOURCE	NOTES	

HD SC 853 320348

SA CA 907 8555

MA-NA-895-100120	100x120mm	N/A	Decal	GR
	25%	N/A	N/A	
HD-SC-853-320348	320x348mm	Semi-Circle	Box	Polished brass padlock
	25%	Recycling bin, Fuda Trading Company	Discarded	
SA-CA-907-8555	85x55mm	N/A	Price tag	Two-sided price display [side 1/2]
	25%	Christodoulakis, H., - Z. Christodoulaki O.E.		

ITEM CODE	SIZE	BRAND	ITEM	USE/APPLICATION
	SCALE	SOURCE	NOTES	

SA-CA-870-215345

SA-JC-937-501200

SA-BL-8004-350240

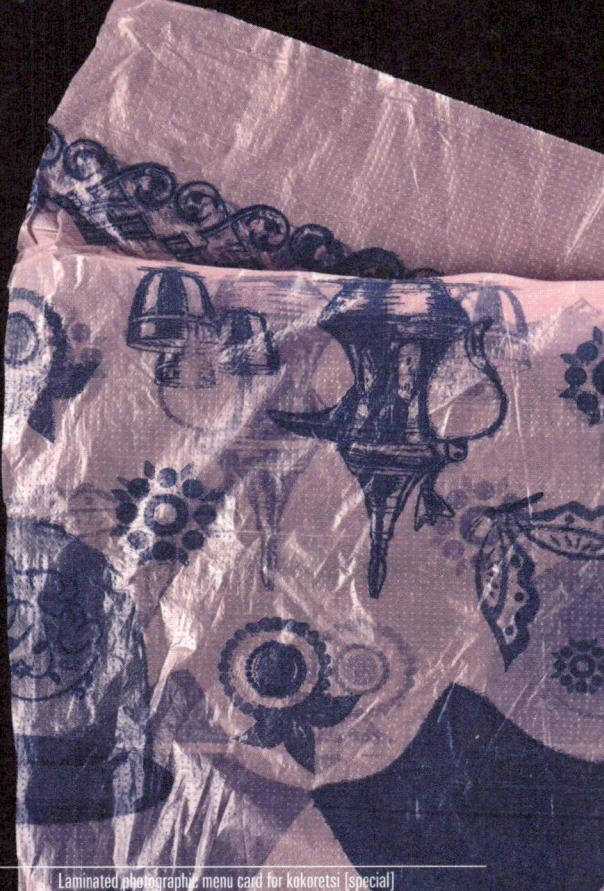

HW-SH-869-330225

SA-CA-870-215345	215x345mm	N/A	Menu Card	Laminated photographic menu card for kokoretsi [special]
	25%	Christodoulakis, H., - Z. Christodoulaki O.E.		
HW-SH-869-330225	330x225mm	Shunjin	Box	Storage bowl with plastic cover. Set of 5
	25%	Recycling bin, Fuda Trading Company	Discarded	
HW-NA-992-3205000	320x5000mm	N/A	Roll	Plastic table cover
	25%	ROJ International Food London	N/A	
SA-JC-937-501200	50x1200mm	Jumbo	Retail Shelf Advertising	Crisps
	25%	N/A	Found on the street	

ITEM CODE	SIZE	BRAND	ITEM	USE / APPLICATION
	SCALE	SOURCE	NOTES	

SA CA 909 8555

SA NA 966 240176

ST NA 002E 13080

SA-CA-909-8555	85x55mm	N/A	Price tag	Two-sided price display [side 2/2]
	25%	Christodoulakis, H., - Z. Christodoulaki O.E.		
ST-NA-002E-13080	130x80mm	N/A	Sticker Set	Color dots [yellow]
	75%	N/A	N/A	
SA-NA-966-240176	240x176mm	N/A	Menu Card	Laminated photographic menu card for gyros
	25%	N/A	Exchanged for artwork	

ITEM CODE	SIZE	BRAND	ITEM	USE / APPLICATION
	SCALE	SOURCE	NOTES	

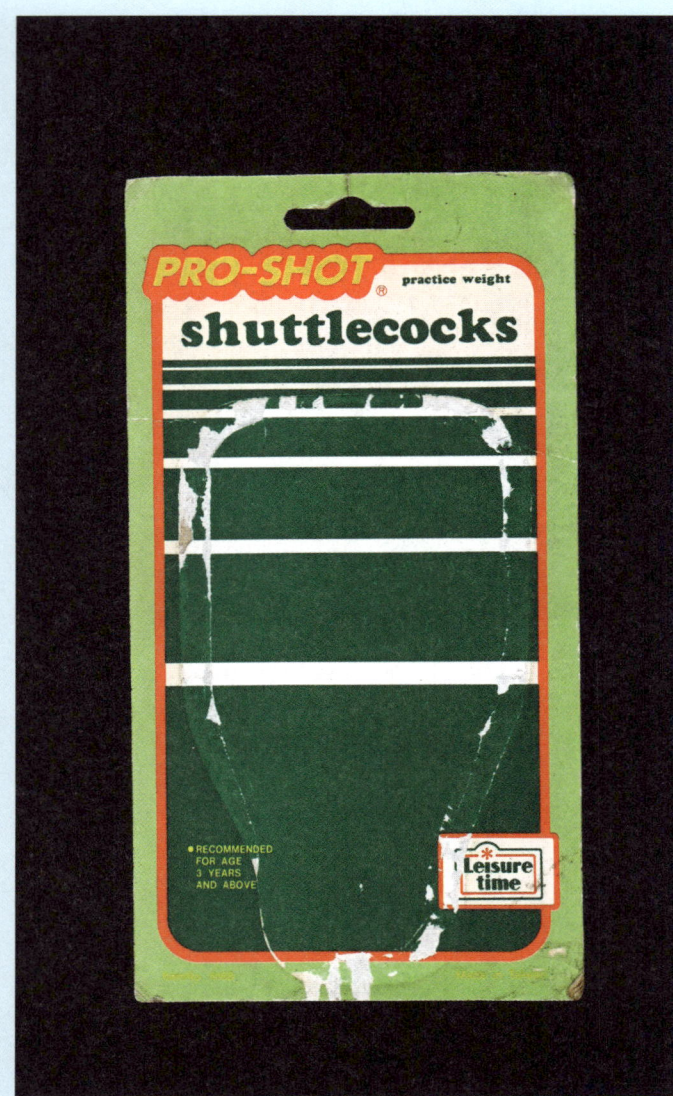

**SA
SF
929
195125**

**SA
CA
909
8555**

**OG
LT
927
226120**

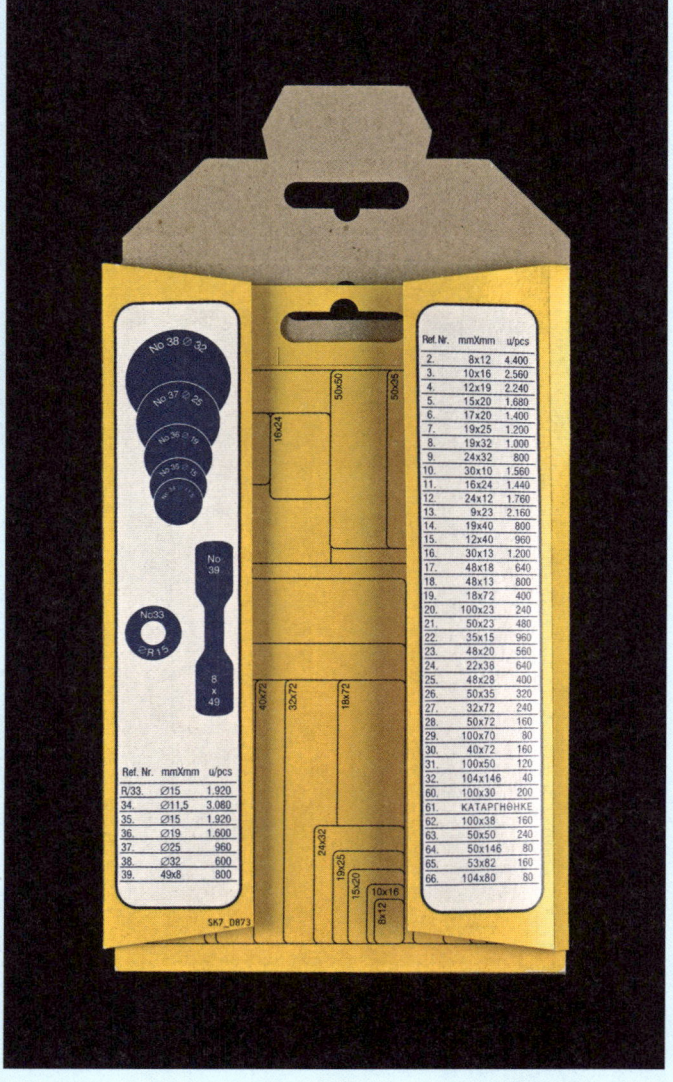

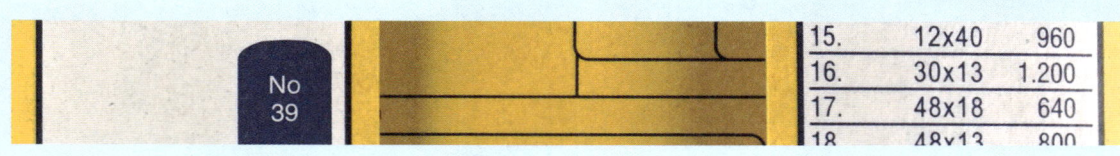

OG-LT-927-226120	226x120 mm	Leisure Time	Packaging	Shuttlecocks
	25%	55 Nigel Road, SET Social	N/A	
SA-CA-909-8555	85x55mm	N/A	Price tag	Two-sided Price display [side 1/2]
	25%	Christodoulakis, H., - Z. Christodoulaki O.E.		
SA-SF-929-195125	195x125mm	Stef-Labels	Packaging	Wholesale package of jewellery labels
	25%	Stoa Kairi	N/A	

Code	Dimensions	Brand	Type	Description
EL-SD-868-357237	357x237mm	SDNMY	Box	High power battery
	25%	Recycling bin, Fuda Trading Company	N/A	
EL-TE-861-265180	265x180mm	T&E	Packaging	Battery pack [22 pieces]
	50%	Kypseli Flea Market	N/A	
EL-TE-893-12030	120x30mm	T&E	Packaging	Alkaline battery set 1.55v
	200%	Galatsi Flea Market	N/A	
HB-ML-939-260164	260x164mm	Mona Liza	Box	Mouline mat-fil embroidery thread
	N/A	N/A	Discarded	
HB-PR-946-240175B	240x175mm	Practice Magazine	Embroidery pattern	Decorating fabric
	25%	Kougeas Used Books	N/A	
HB-PR-946-594841	594x841mm	Practice Magazine	Embroidery pattern	Romantic white clothing [folded]
	N/A	Kougeas Used Books	N/A	
HB-WH-958-240175A	240x175mm	The Woman and the Home [magazine]	Embroidery Pattern [folded]	Decorating fabric
	25%	Stathmos Old Books Store	N/A	
HD-AR-921-100100	100x100mm	ARMATOOL	Packaging	N/A
	75%	Epidavros, GR	Made in Japan	
HD-BA-885-5035D	50x35mm	Basic	N/A	N/A
	25%	HSDS Studio	Gifted	
HD-CI-864-240138	240x138mm	Cimberio	Box	P.T.F.E. Threadsealing
	25%	Exarchia Flea Market	Discarded	
HD-NA-8004-38035A	380x35mm	N/A	Packaging	Mounting tape
	50%	55 Nigel Road, SET Social	Discarded	
HD-NA-8806-80435F	80x435mm	N/A	Packaging	Nylon cable ties
	25%	N/A	Discarded	
HD-NA-901-180100	180x100mm	N/A	Box	2 in 1 Scale and Tape Measure
	25%	Kiosk	Discarded	
HD-NA-940-145124	145x124mm	Fischer	Paper bag [part of]	Hardware store
	100%	Rekkas Angeliki	Discarded	
HD-NH-7990-5030E	50x30mm	New Holland	Packaging	N/A
	50%	N/A	Discarded	
HD-SC-853-320348	320x348mm	Semi-Circle	Box	Polished brass padlock
	25%	Recycling bin, Fuda Trading Company	Discarded	
HD-SU-8006-240180B	240x180mm	Supreme	Packaging	Flooring Trims
	25%	55 Nigel Road, SET Social	Discarded	
HD-VE-924-310247	310x247mm	VESSEL	Packaging	Screwdrivers
	N/A	Mitropoulos, V., & Co. Ltd	Discarded	
HW-AK-866-350220	350x220mm	AKA	Box lid	Packaging for door handles
	25%	Bardis	Donated after attempt of theft	
HW-EN-924-148105	148x105mm	ENERGY	Product Label	Element from car sponge wrapping
	50%	N/A	European Product	
HW-HA-965-260163	260x163mm	HAOHUI	Packaging backing	Stainless steel scourers
	25%	Exarchia Flea Market	Found on the street	
HW-HE-011-1401035	140x103x58mm	HENG-GUAN	Packaging	Small night light
	25%	Kypseli Flea Market	Front and back	
HW-NA-7972-279215	279x215mm	N/A	Signage	For sale
	N/A	7th Ave Copy & Office Supplies	N/A	
HW-NA-992-3205000	320x5000mm	N/A	Roll	Plastic table cover
	25%	ROJ International Food London	N/A	
HW-SH-869-330225	330x225mm	Shunjin	Box	Storage bowl with plastic cover. Set of 5
	25%	Recycling bin, Fuda Trading Company	Discarded	
HW-TO-7914-260110	260x110mm	Topmaster	Packaging	Triangular steel file
	25%	N/A	N/A	
MA-AR-7990-3560D	35x60mm	Arrow	Sticker	Promotional
	50%	Dianele Gianetti	Gifted	
MA-DI-854-145390	145x390mm	D.I.D.	Packaging	Motorbike chain 525VX3
	100%	Henry Stringer	Gifted	
MA-HO-977-70560K	70x560mm	Honda	Decal	Astrea Supra
	50%	Tourtoglou Prodromos	N/A	
MA-NA-895-100120	100x120mm	N/A	Decal	GR
	25%	N/A	N/A	
MA-NA-974-145158	145x158mm	N/A	Decal	Number for motorbike
	25%	Tourtoglou Prodromos	N/A	
MA-NA-986-340090	340x90mm	N/A	Decal	Wheel reflective pinstripe tape
	N/A	Car.gr	N/A	
MA-NA-987-1501130	150x1130mm	N/A	Decal	Motorbike
	50%	Tourtoglou Prodromos	N/A	
MA-UF-7990-4060B	40x60 mm	Ultra Firenze	Sticker	Promotional
	50%	Dianele Gianetti	Gifted	
MA-YA-981-105230	105x230mm	N/A	Decal	Yamaha XT
	100%	Tourtoglou Prodromos	N/A	
MA-YO-863-250195	250x195mm	YOKOHAMA	Box	Packaging for motorbike battery
	25%	Epidavros, GR	Donated by Lefki Varangi	
OG-BO-902-2395F	23x95mm	BOOSTER	Packaging	Cut out from firework product
	N/A	Burgess Park	Donated by Daniel Gatenio	

ID	Size / %	Brand / Source	Type / Note	Description
OG-HE-891-5580	55x80mm	Henbrandt Ltd	Packaging	Fun Snaps
	25%	Khan's Bargains	Not for sale to persons under 16	
OG-LT-927-226120	226x120mm	Leisure Time	Packaging	Shuttlecocks
	25%	55 Nigel Road, SET Social	N/A	
OG-MJ-926-25090	250x90mm	Major Value	Packaging	Garden pruning shears
	25%	55 Nigel Road, SET Social	Discarded	
OG-NA-867-250180	250x180mm	N/A	Product Label	Tour Mat
	25%	N/A	Donated by Greg & Clara	
SA-BL-8004-13078	130x78mm	Blick	Sticker Set	Postal
	100%	Lasheen The Stationer	N/A	
SA-CA-870-215345	215x345mm	N/A	Menu Card	Laminated photographic menu card for kokoretsi [special]
	25%	Christodoulakis, H., - Z. Christodoulaki O.E.		
SA-CA-903-8555	85x55mm	N/A	Price tag	Two-sided price display [side 1/2]
	25%	Christodoulakis, H., - Z. Christodoulaki O.E.		
SA-CA-907-8555	85x55mm	N/A	Price tag	Two-sided price display [side 1/2]
	25%	Christodoulakis, H., - Z. Christodoulaki O.E.		
SA-CA-909-8555	85x55mm	N/A	Price tag	Two-sided price display [side 2/2]
	25%	Christodoulakis, H., - Z. Christodoulaki O.E.		
SA-CA-909-8555	85x55mm	N/A	Price tag	Two-sided Price display [side 1/2]
	25%	Christodoulakis, H., - Z. Christodoulaki O.E.		
SA-JC-937-501200	50x1200mm	Jumbo	Retail Shelf Advertising	Crisps
	25%	N/A	Found on the street	
SA-LE-3871-360250	360x250mm	VANG TRANS-RASTER	Lettraset	Dry-transfer lettering for architectural plans
	N/A	PALLI [Art and Design Supplies]	N/A	
SA-NA-8004-130105F	130x105mm	N/A	Sticker Set	Postal
	100%	N/A	N/A	
SA-NA-8004-313080C	130x80mm	N/A	Sticker Set	Diamond Shaped
	25%	N/A	N/A	
SA-NA-8004-8463D	84x63mm	N/A	Sticker Set	Arrows
	50%	N/A	N/A	
SA-NA-966-240176	240x176mm	N/A	Menu Card	Laminated photographic menu card for gyros
	25%	N/A	Exchanged for artwork	
SA-SF-929-195125	195x125mm	Stef-Labels	Packaging	Wholesale package of jewellery labels
	25%	Stoa Kairi	N/A	
SA-SL-002D-130107	130x107mm	Stef-Labels	Price Tags	Jewellery Labels
	100%	Stoa Kairi	Made in Hellas	
SA-SL-925-195125	195x125mm	Stef-Labels	Packaging [back of]	Wholesale package of jewellery labels
	25%	Stoa Kairi	Made in Hellas	
SA-WS-923-26570B	265x70mm	N/A	Plastic Bag [part of]	Wholesale product for tourist shops
	25%	N/A	Acquired while shopping	
ST-BI-8006-350240A	350x240mm	Bindermax	Packaging	Plastic index tabs
	25%	Egglezos Vafeiadakis	Sourced at Legal Stationery Shop	
ST-BL-896-13090	130x90mm	Blick	Packaging	Office stickers
	50%	Bright Printers & Stationers	Discarded	
ST-BL-897-13090	130x90mm	N/A	Packaging	Labels
	25%	Bright Printers & Stationers	Made in Denmark	
ST-HE-8004-10584A	105x84mm	Vario Hermia	Sticker Set	Numbering
	100%	VIVLIOCHARTIKI Ltd.	N/A	
ST-HE-8004-400240B	400x240mm	Vario Hermia	Sticker Set	Color dots
	N/A	SMART OFFICE SUPPLIES I.K.E	N/A	
ST-HE-8004-83120C	83x120mm	N/A	Sticker Set	Arrows
	100%	SMART OFFICE SUPPLIES I.K.E	N/A	
ST-LI-859-250175	250x175mm	Lion Triangles	Triangular paper envelope	Set square set
	75%	N/A	N/A	
ST-NA-002A-13080	130x80mm	N/A	Sticker Set	Numbered labels
	25%	N/A	N/A	
ST-NA-002B-10770	107x70mm	N/A	Sticker Set	Postal
	100%	N/A	Final request	
ST-NA-002C-13080	130x80mm	N/A	Sticker Set	Postal
	25%	N/A	N/A	
ST-NA-002E-13080	130x80mm	N/A	Sticker Set	Color dots [yellow]
	75%	N/A	N/A	
ST-NA-8006-13080C	130x80mm	N/A	Sticker Set	Numbers [black]
	50%	Bright Printers & Stationers	N/A	
ST-NA-8006-350240E	350x240mm	N/A	Sticker Set	Color dots [orange]
	50%	Kim's Newsagent	N/A	
ST-NA-883-4040	40x40mm	N/A	Sticker	Metallic prize
	25%	Bright Printers & Stationers	N/A	
ST-NA-892-5035R	50x35mm	N/A	Sticker	Greek alphabet
	50%	N/A	N/A	
ST-NA-895-15090	150x90mm	Super Initial HK	Sticker in package	Vinyl sticker
	25%	Lucas Dupuy	Gifted	
ST-NA-895-15090B	150x90mm	Super Initial HK	Sticker in package	Vinyl sticker
	25%	Lucas Dupuy	Gifted	

Use by:
How to use:
Caution
Do not use
Directions of use:
Mix
Contents:
Shake well
Easy to install
With plastic cover
All figures
Are approximate
Whatever you need
Sticks on
Almost anything
Job Done!

The Commodity and the Exhibition
Joshua Simon

It is perfectly understandable that the dandy, the man who is never ill at ease, would be the ideal of a society that had begun to experience a bad conscience with respect to objects. What compelled the noblest names of England, and the regent himself, to hang on every word that fell from Beau Brummell's lips was the fact that he presented himself as the master of science that they could not do without. To men who had lost their self-possession, the dandy, who makes of elegance and the superfluous his raison d'être, teaches the possibility of a new relation to things, which goes beyond both the enjoyment of their use-value and the accumulation of their exchange value. He is the redeemer of things, the one who wipes out, with his elegance, their original sin: the commodity.

— Giorgio Agamben, *Stanzas: Word and Phantasm in Western Culture*

In addition to critiques of the market and of the cycles of exploitation enacted by commodity exchange, a new set of sensibilities has recently been introduced in contemporary art that are concerned with how the commodity and its surrounding economy activate us. Based on this new sensibility, the exhibition becomes a format that enables us to see the commodity as it is. Therefore, one can say that the commodity is really only true to itself as art. The suspended existence of exhibits on display provides for the commodity's nature to appear beyond a specific exchange, use, and sign values. But in order to understand objects, we must first acknowledge that every artwork is first and foremost a commodity.

In his three-part essay, "Art and Thingness", Sven Lütticken examines the art object as a transient object subjected to commodification through a series of processes of fetishization and abstraction.[1] Lütticken's demonstration of a shift in the object is one of the many virtues of the text: "'Things' are no longer passively waiting for a concept, theory, or sovereign subject to arrange them in ordered ranks of objecthood."[2] To my mind, however, this impressive survey neglects to examine the commodity as an entity prior to the art object — or rather, as the thing that precedes any object, including art objects.

The exhibition framework facilitates a form of seeing that allows the encounter of contemporary art objects as a commodity. Even when artists, curators, critics, and spectators opt for an intimate, narrative, symbolic, critical, or alternative understanding of objects, objects in an exhibition nevertheless converse in the language of commodities. While formal analysis reveals that this nonliteral language involves materials, colors, shapes, scale, and composition, we may wonder: what exactly do objects say?

In the section of *Capital* entitled "The Fetishism of Commodities and the Secret Thereof," Karl Marx demonstrates that the commodity is a materialization of our social relations:

A commodity appears, at first sight, an extremely obvious, trivial thing. But its analysis brings out that it is a very strange thing, abounding in metaphysical subtleties and theological niceties. So far as it is a use-value, there is nothing mysterious about it, whether we consider it from the point of view that by its properties it satisfies human needs, or that it first takes on these properties as the product of human labor. It is absolutely clear that, by his activity, man changes the forms of the materials of nature in such a way to make them useful to him. The form of wood, for instance, is altered if a table is made out of it. Nevertheless, the table continues to be wood, an ordinary sensuous thing. But as soon as it emerges as a commodity, it changes into a thing which transcends sensuousness. It not only stands with its feet on the ground, but, in relation to all other commodities, it stands on its head, and evolves out of its wooden brain grotesque ideas, far more wonderful than if it were to begin dancing of its own free will.[3]

According to Marx, the commodity is comprised of two values: use value and exchange value. The commodity is the thing that always feels at home. Whereas man suffers from a folkloric and identity-dependent conception of foreignness, acquaintance, history, tradition, and alienation, and plants and animals have difficulty acclimating, the commodity is a mode of being that is free of all these. It is first and foremost a presence.

Their World, Not Ours

It may be that in the near future we will be able to discuss this civilization of private property in the past tense but for now it is present in all its

---

1   See Sven Lütticken, "Art and Thingness, Part One: Breton's Ball and Duchamp's Carrot," *e-flux journal*, no. 13 (February 2010); "Art and Thingness, Part Two: Thingification," *e-flux journal*, no. 15 (April 2010); and "Art and Thingness, Part Three: The Heart of the Thing is the Thing We Don't Know," *e-flux journal*, no. 16 (May 2010).
2   Lütticken, "Art and Thingness, Part One." See also Mitchell, *What Do Pictures Want?*, 112.
3   Karl Marx, "The Fetishism of Commodities and the Secret Thereof," in *Capital*, vol. 1, *A Critique of Political Economy*, trans. Ben Fowkes (London: Penguin Books, 1992), 163. At the conference "One Divides into Two: Dialectics, Negativity & Clinamen" at the Institute for Cultural Inquiry, Berlin (March 28–30, 2011), Slavoj Žižek, in his lecture "Hegel As a Critic of Marx," pointed out that this famous description of the commodity does not follow a simple empiricist scenario by which a transcendent entity is unveiled as a trivial everyday thing, but rather the opposite: Marx proposes the commodity, which appears to be a mundane and common thing, to be abounding in metaphysical subtleties.

extremes. Private property remains the cornerstone of an all-encompassing concept of our civilization, and it is the key to understanding our relations with each other and with things, as well as the relationships between things themselves. It is important to recognize that the commodity is a conceptual framework based on negation, on exclusion — something can be mine only if it excludes anyone else who might possibly possess it. Once we realize that our notion of property is based on negation, we learn its harsh consequences — we are actually the ones excluded from the property we think we own. By excluding others we follow the logic of negation which operates at the basis of our social relations with people and things. Therefore, the logic of ownership that has guided our understanding of the world of things never rises to the task of actually describing our relations with them. Most commodities live longer than their creators and consumers alike—for even a simple plastic bag will outlive us all many times over. As commodities ourselves, even our bodily organs can outlive us. Therefore, as all objects that enter into this world are commodities, we must realize that this is not our world, but theirs. We dwell in the world of commodities and, what's more, in the commodities' world.

Private property is the basic category of our civilization, and it is through inheritance that private property is passed on, thus creating its own history of civilization. Freedom from property — and, by extension, inheritance — can free us from this history and present the prospect of a new civilization, with the relation to and between objects existing as a primary anchor. For the purposes of tracing our understanding of objects today, it is important to understand the category of private property as an insufficient one.

A well-known advertisement by luxury wristwatchmaker Patek Philippe seems to suggest a way to break open the paradox of ownership and inheritance by identifying the explicit tension between the existence of the object and the ownership of it: "You never actually own a Patek Philippe. You merely look after it for the next generation."[4] By consecrating inheritance, the advertisement asserts that nothing can be owned — only looked after.

Not only can we no longer believe in the myth of ownership, but we also require a new ethics for communicating with objects — for taking care, looking after, and watching over them.

By pushing for an ethics where inheritance is the reason for taking care of things — we care for them to benefit our dynasties, our networks, to keep them as an object that we, in some way, own — the Patek Philippe ad allows a glimpse into the core of this value system: we actually own nothing. Ownership is an economic speculation. If anything, this relation to things calls for a new ethics that impels us to take care of things so that they can no longer be private property; this prioritizes sentimental value over exchange, use, and sign values.[5]

Commodities present a different way into history. If we examine historical events from the perspective of the commodity, they reveal an alternate history. For example, we find that the French Revolution, as an expression of a revolutionary demand for private property to answer the bourgeois call "Laissez passer! Laissez faire!" was also a demand for the free passage of commodities through trade. In the spirit of the *Declaration of the Rights of Man and of the Citizen*, in which private property is a sanctified right according to Article XVII, commodities blow with the wind, and every place is their home.[6] Unlike people, commodities (and not only in the form of cars, trains, and airplanes) are allowed smoother, and quicker, passage.

Another example can be found in the European Union (EU), which we usually regard as dating back to the European Economic Community, inaugurated through a series of treaties after World War II. But if we revisit the events during and following World War II, we find that, contrary to the common belief that the unification of Europe started with the Treaties of Rome in 1957 — signed by the leaders of France, West Germany, Italy, Belgium, the Netherlands, and Luxembourg as a result of the scars of the war — the union was born, from the perspective of the commodity, in the Vichy government's collaboration with the Nazis in June 1940, when France and Germany worked together for the first time after generations of hostility.

While part of France was occupied by the Nazis, another part was collaborating with them, and consequently customs regulations between occupied France and Germany changed. With the end of World War II, this state of affairs simply continued. Thus, the commodity teaches us history — its provocative truth is that the EU starts with and is a continuation of the collaboration between the Nazis and the Vichy France.[7]

---

4 I thank Noam Yuran for drawing my attention to this advertisement.
5 With sentimental value, I know I am using a loaded term that is often synonymous with fetish. For example, the attraction to "vintage" relates to a demand from the thing to hold and materialize former uses and cultural meanings. My use of the term is different and relates to its commodity nature.
6 See Georges Lefebvre, "The Bourgeois Revolution," in *The French Revolution*, vol. 1, trans. Elizabeth Moss Evanson (New York: Columbia University Press, 1962), 102–16.
7 The economic policies of privatizations and austerity under the regulations of the EU and the European Central Bank are also to be read in a broader context of the Nazi economic restructuring. Writing on the French takeover of British power plants since Margaret Thatcher's restructuring of the electricity industry in the 1980s in the United Kingdom, James Meek mentions the first usage of the word "privatization" in the English language: Privatization was not a Thatcher patent. The Spanish economist Germà Bel traces the origins of the word to the German word *Reprivatisierung*, first used in the English in 1936 by the Berlin correspondent of the *Economist*, writing about Nazi economic policy. In 1943, in an analysis of Hitler's programme in the *Quarterly Journal of Economics*, the word "privatization" entered the academic literature for the first time. The author, Sidney Merlin, wrote that the Nazi Party "facilitates the accumulation of private fortunes and industrial empires by its foremost members and collaborators through 'privatization' and other measures, thereby intensifying centralization of economic affairs and government in an increasingly narrow group that may for all practical purposes be termed the national socialist elite." James Meek, "How We Happened to Sell Off Our Electricity," *London Review of Books* 34, no. 17 (September 13, 2012): 3–4.

Products & Services

Pier Paolo Pasolini's film in *La rabbia* (1963), especially the original cut released in 2008 by Giuseppe Bertolucci as *La rabbia di Pasolini*, gives an account of this.[8] In it we see a newsreel of the early stages of the European Economic Community and hear the reporter say: "the first solid results did not take long to appear: on 10 February 1953 the first coal train crossed the French-German border freely; in May of the same year the first European steel was cast by the steelworks in Luxembourg." Pasolini's voice-over adds: "the Common Market will come, meanwhile we dance the common dance, the Fascist Petty-Bourgeois is ready for European Unity."

And insofar as people now have free passage, they are doomed to follow the path of commodities. Individuals receive right of passage either as members of a workforce or as tourists. The familiar question "business or pleasure?" comes to stand for the limited categories within which movement is understood in the world — in both cases it is work.

As we have already seen, everything that comes into this world does so as a commodity. This world belongs to the commodity, not to us. And today it would be difficult to deny that we have more intimate relations with commodities than we do with each other. On a social level, the commodity can be considered part of a networked economy of exploitation: from design and creation, through marketing and distribution, to consumption and waste. According to Marxist tradition, the fetishistic treatment of commodities empties them of meaning, hiding the social relations that were invested in them through human labor. This allows imaginary, ideological, and symbolic social relations to be, in Sut Jhally's terms, "injected into the construction of meaning."[9] Jhally maps the new meanings that advertising produces through commodity fetishism in four successive religious stages: (1) utility/idolatry, in which commodities are freed from being merely utilitarian things; (2) symbolization/iconology, in which commodities serve as abstract representations of social values; (3) personification/narcissism, in which they are intimately connected with the world of interpersonal relations; and (4) lifestyle/totemism, in which the first three stages merge to define the group under a singular lifestyle.[10]

Commodities as carriers of social values are scripted as such to an extent that one does not really have a clue who he or she is — that is, without the brands one is loyal to. Money is the ultimate representational system of value in this civilization. Marx has demonstrated that it is through the objective symbol of monetary value that commodity fetishism conceals labor and thus social relations. According to Marx, the commodity must have human labor invested in it. Marx's argument seems to suggest that we are actually a materialization of commodities' relations.[11] But although it is the actual materialization of social relations, the commodity, be it goods or services, fetishizes itself through the equivalence of monetary value, presenting itself as a relation between objects — kicking humans out of the equation, so to speak.

In spite of the fact that the producer's labor is the source of the commodities' value, within the context of the market, the producer thinks of the fruit of his or her own labor as a consumer would: as objects to be bought and sold. While they may still be this, they also have a social life of their own that has included us in it.[12] In this way, the commodity fetish echoes the workers' silence. As David Harvey puts it, "capital is not a thing, but rather a process in which money is perpetually sent in search of more money."[13] As an object, then, the commodity materializes labor as capital and operates as both thing and process. The universality of money is easily exchanged for the particularity of the commodity. But when the commodity's particularity must be converted into the universality of money, things become much more problematic: desire and need have to come into play in order for the commodity to be absorbed.[14] The drive of the fetish has to work its magic as well. Interestingly enough, the commodity actually loses its monetary value at the moment of payment — as soon as the commodity is purchased, it is on its way to becoming waste. As long as money is converted into commodities (universality into particularity) the issue of value is simple, but when commodities have to be converted into money (particularity into universality), the drive that was there with the fetish — the use, exchange, and sign value — changes. In the end we are left with sentimental value, which enables a real examination of the thing that

---

8   This film attempts to reconstruct the complete version of Pasolini's segment which was distributed by producer Gastone Ferranti together with a more conservative take by filmmaker Giovannino Guareschi under the title *La rabbia*.
9   Sut Jhally, *The Codes of Advertising: Fetishism and the Political Economy of Meaning in the Consumer Society* (New York: Psychology Press, 1990), 51.
10 Ibid., 201–2.
11 This opens up the possibility to recognize the sentimental value materialized in the commodity. For example, in the cultural capitalism of "social networks," social relationality is the commodity. "In 'immaterial labor,' 'relations between people' are 'not so much hidden beneath the veneer of objectivity, but are themselves the very material of our everyday exploitation.'" Slavoj Žižek quoting Nina Power. Slavoj Žižek, "How to Begin from the Beginning," in *The Idea of Communism*, 221
12 See for example Arjun Appadurai's notion of the anthropology of things in "Commodities and the Politics of Value," in *The Social Life of Things: Commodities in Cultural Perspective*, ed. Arjun Appadurai (Cambridge: Cambridge University Press, 1986), 3–64. Appadurai also suggests that the object is not only evidence but also a witness. A recent conceptualization along the lines of this was brought forward by Thomas Keenan and Eyal Weizman in their collaborative book *Mengele's Skull*. In it, the authors claim with regards toward crime investigations, several narrative shifts have been made since World War II. According to Keenan and Weizman, these investigations moved from the framework of the document (e.g., the Nuremberg Trials) to that of the witness (e.g., the Eichmann Trial) to what they call "Forensic Aesthetics" in which objects themselves are summoned to testify and speak. This third narrative, they hold, was born with the investigation on the authenticity of Josef *Mengele's skull* in Brazil in 1985. See Thomas Keenan and Eyal Weizman, *Mengele's Skull: The Advent of a Forensic Aesthetics* (Berlin: Sternberg Press, 2012), 12–13.
13 David Harvey, *The Enigma of Capital and The Crises of Capitalism* (Oxford: Oxford University Press, 2010), 40.
14 Ibid., 106.

Products & Services

outlives us; the actual thing that came into the world as a commodity.

But in a consumer economy in which we are faced with more commodities than human beings, can we still believe that commodities are solely a mere materializations of our social relations? Consider our physical bodies: a conglomeration of blood sugar levels, kidney stones, cholesterol levels, or cancerous pollution. Our bodies and the breakdown of physical processes come from our consumption — of sugars and minerals, of proteins and toxins. In our relations with commodities, we no longer have the ability to decide between production or consumption, intent or mistake, improvisation or function, profit or loss. It is in this way that, as part of the social relations that materialize within it, the commodity gains a life of its own beyond even the means of its invention: design, manufacturing, production, marketing, shipment, disposal, and evacuation.

The Exhibition

As a practice of conceptualizing singularities, the curatorial produces the viewing tools through which to be seen. The exhibition has a relative quality like any narrative — *I see one thing in this while you see another*. It also has a relational quality as an event — scripted and unscripted relations between the various authors of a piece, the worlds the piece connects, the ones of the space and its context add, the curated syntax, and the world which the viewers bring forth. In addition to its relative and relational qualities it has as a narrative and event, the exhibition is characterized by a certain concentration generated by a suspended duration of being among objects. In addition, the exhibition is also a form of exiting. As soon as you enter an exhibition space, you walk through it as if you were on your way out. In this sense, the exhibition and the commodity share an allegorical relation.

In his seminal 1967 essay "Art and Objecthood," Michael Fried recognized the Minimalist (or "literalist," in his terminology) object's tendency toward anthropomorphism. It is an art object that aspires to have a presence in the space equal to that of the viewer: "Literalist art stakes everything on shape as a given property of objects, if not indeed as a kind of object in its own right. It aspires not to defeat or suspend its own objecthood, but on the contrary to discover and project objecthood as such."[15] Paradoxically, it is the critical tools used by formalists (and those leaning toward mysticism of all things) that allow for an entry point into the language of things. As art, it is agreed that objects speak — with us and between themselves. The neomaterialist investigation can use the formalist discussion, which revolves around questions on materials, shapes, volume, scale, composition, texture, effect, and authorship, only by actualizing the commodity character of the object. But at the end of the day, literalist/Minimalist attempts keep with the logic of cause and effect; they tell us that the artist created an object that aspires to an equal presence to that of the viewer. Minimalism is anthropocentric, but commodities are everywhere and they show themselves to be prior to the viewer and to the artist — they are not only art, but also art.

Objects in an exhibition are characterized by a suspended duration of being, allowing them to exist beyond use, exchange, and even sign value.

When we wish to describe what is being exhibited, we usually use the words "object," "piece," "artifact," "thing," "product," and even "commodity." One's preference depends on the discourse to which the description belongs. "Object" is used commonly in contemporary art, as it is regarded as intrinsically constitutive of subjects — for example, in Hebrew, "object" means "will" (*chefetz* — similar to "having an objective" in English). "Piece" is also common in this context, as it introduces a maker as the master of that piece and suggests that the thing is passive and transparent, a mere projection of its maker's intention. "Thing" is used mainly in relation to a mute presence that calls for contextualization. "Product" refers to a process of creation, bringing with it an impression of finality, a fait accompli. And "artifact" relates to an outcome or a residue. "Commodity" is used primarily in the context of a critique of the market, but I believe that this term should include all of the definitions mentioned above.[16]

In our prefabricated world, one can claim that all things are commodities:objects, land, air, garbage, debt, action, and so forth. In a world where everything is already a commodity, "object" and "thing" are in this respect terms that attempt to cleanse the commodity of the chains of its birth, thus hiding its history and the means by which it appears in the world. As both a retinal and non-retinal viewing mechanism, the exhibition embodies a much wider aesthetic experience that allows us to view commodities as they are. More than in any other context, commodities are most true to themselves as art.

---

15 Michael Fried, "Art and Objecthood," in *Art and Objecthood: Essays and Reviews* (Chicago: University of Chicago Press, 1996), 151.
16 My aim here is to preserve the Marxian notion that to some extent the commodity has a mind of its own and that this "mind" is actually what we see in the exhibition. For a critical analysis of use value and exchange value, as well as fetishism in relation to labor, see the chapter "Fetishism and Ideology" in Jean Baudrillard, *For a Critique of the Political Economy of the Sign*, trans. Charles Levin (New York: Telos, 1981), 88–101. For a discussion of various "pure" and "loose" definitions of the commodity between exchange and value, see Appadurai, "Commodities and the Politics of Value," 3–64.

SDNMY
POWERDAGK
EVEREADY
SUZ
High visability
Patent Pending
Etc
Nigh
5D
6D
Decore
NRG
Packsge
Styl
Pefrectc
Vessel

Great for all
Simply
Suitable
For most materials
Quality approved
First class materials
Anyways
do tests before
Instructions
Figure 1
Figure 2
Like this
Not like this
Applications:
Ideal for:
Basic Needs

Changing Display

Lisa Sudhibhasilp

The North

The Boven 't Y shopping centre—translatable as 'above the IJ river'—is situated on Buikslotermeerplein in Amsterdam North. Opening its doors in 1970, it was initially surrounded by endless fields and farms. Today, the area has transformed into a densely urbanised landscape featuring apartment towers, social housing, a retirement home complex, a hospital, a cinema, the 'ring' highway, and notably, the metro. Throughout the years, the shopping centre has undergone various phases of renovation or, in a more optimistic tone, revitalisation. Despite changes to its infrastructure, the layout and low-rise shops have remained the same since the '70s. Conceived between a pedestrian mall and a strip mall, it houses two major competing food supermarkets, a McDonald's, snack bars, home improvement stores, and numerous unbranded, affordable fashion clothing shops.

Construction site for the Buikslotermeerplein shopping centre, 1967, Archief van de Dienst Ruimtelijke Ordening en rechtsvoorganger, Stadsarchief Amsterdam

In 2019, I came to the Boven 't Y for the first time to visit a potential studio space for rent. My initial impression was of encountering a strange blend of outdated and modern elements in both architecture and urban planning. The North-South metro line had just started operating, finally connecting this part of the city to the centre.

The new metro line resulted in a quick expansion of the urban area, marked by taller and fancier buildings – just like another New Jersey facing another New York City. The North evolved from industrial buildings, large windy roads and vacant lots to a condominium paradise and its spacious bars and restaurants catering to the younger crowd and expat families of three. The surrounding area underwent this rapid transformation, far outpacing the so-called revitalisation efforts of the shopping centre.

Therefore, in 2019, much like trespassing in a haunted mall, I recall the numerous vacant shops still advertised at high rents, surrounded by outdated stores selling unwanted items. One of these empty shops became my studio, shared with other artists. We could rent it for the minimum, covering only the operating costs, until a new – and legitimate – tenant would appear. We were there as a transition to fill the gap and prevent the space from decaying. We served as legal squatters, conveniently replaceable with a one-month notice.

The Bank

The studio was a former Rabobank, now an empty 140m2, two-story, long and narrow space. Inside, only wood-printed vinyl flooring remained, along with a false ceiling, its built-in LED lights, and free-standing power socket towers. Some traces persisted from its former function: the ATMs, now rectangles filled with concrete and closed with MDF panels, marks on the floor from the thick walls of the vault, and the bullet-proof slot at the back for passing money. The front entrance was an automatic sliding door that we had to disconnect after entering to keep it closed for the curious passers-by. A staircase illuminated from underneath led to a brown-carpeted first floor, divided into small rooms with glass walls and doors, pretending to make today's finances more transparent. It was ironic to think and produce art in a place that once distributed cash or refused mortgages.

The connection between art and money is undeniable, yet art is often idealised as transcending its trivial necessities. Therefore we tend to hide or embellish the economic realities and labour involved in its creation. This studio in the former bank was a symbolic reminder of this artifice in a quite cynical way. And this ironic shift of function was not an isolated case but a rather current and common Neo-liberal phenomenon.

Nederlandse Middenstands Bank in Amsterdam Noord (Buikslotermeerplein), 1974, Fotocollectie Anefo, Hans Peters, Nationaal Archief

In 2010, squatting became illegal in the Netherlands, leading to Anti-kraak (Anti-squatting) as an alternative. Under this new legislation, through vacant property management companies, owners could place individuals or businesses in empty buildings at a low rent and with limited tenant rights, to supposedly protect properties. Spaces are now interchangeable and temporary, resulting in nomadic and precarious lifestyles. It became commonplace to encounter pop-up stores in churches or temples, artist studios in offices, night clubs in schools, or art galleries in factories.

Buikslotermeerplein, Archief van de Dienst Ruimtelijke, 1973, Stadsarchief Amsterdam

The Deal

There were in total six artist studios in Boven 't Y. Our arrangement was part of an anti-squatting agreement organised by an art institution that was planning to open its doors in a nearby building. At that time, their strategy to offer culture to the neighbourhood started by bringing art raw material: artists. We were then "placed" in these vacant shops with the implicit promise to the shop owners that we would visually enhance the somewhat dreary shopping centre by displaying art in the windows and perhaps even engaging in some grand painting gestures visible from the pedestrian walkways. In reality, our studios looked like storage spaces rather than carefully curated painting workshops.

The cohabitation in the shopping centre exposed the unspoken rule of displaying ourselves and our activity, aligning with the meticulous merchandising efforts of our neighbours' windows. For Boven 't Y, our presence was a decorative temporary solution for the (too) many vacant stores, while, for the art institution, it served as a tool of gentrification under the promise of bridging the local community with culture. This disparity in expectations was resolved by placing giant artwork stickers on the store windows, blocking views from the shoppers but allowing us to see outside.

It is evident that the artist-as-gentrifier plays a significant role in this narrative. However, artists serve as both protagonists and victims, often passive in the process of gentrification, ultimately responsible for their own future eviction. While often sought to revitalise low-income areas, they paradoxically become commodities, generating value they themselves cannot afford.

The large and cheap studios offered to us became the very force that eventually swallowed us up, forcing us to retreat to even more distant peripheries.

The Back Door

Hidden behind the giant sticker, I reflected on working in this peculiar context. I would imagine the bank's clients sitting where I moulded plaster or cut particle boards. I remember observing shoppers as my preferred procrastinating activity, recognising some of them as regulars. There was, for instance, an elderly woman in an automatic wheelchair who always fed pigeons in front of our locked sliding door, mistakenly believing it was another abandoned store.

My cigarette breaks were taken in the back, allowing me to observe other workers doing the same behind their respective stores. The shopping centre was designed in a way that these back areas were out of the shoppers' sight, reserved for employee parking and garbage collection. It wasn't a pleasant place, nor was it intended to be. Our back doors led to this sacred and secret territory thought to be only practical, lacking comfort compared to the front alleys with their squares, benches, potted flowers, and even an ongoing faded background music.

Shopping centres embody a space and time for leisure, designed for relaxation and idleness. They are also environments where excessive consumption is promoted, a behaviour that might otherwise be discouraged. Contradictory, it is in the back areas where one finds the real respite from hard work, where the waste is revealed, and the support network apparent.

Buikslotermeerplein, Archief van de Dienst Ruimtelijke, 1971, Stadsarchief Amsterdam

Products & Services

Winkelcentrum Buikslotermeerplein, Amsterdam Noord, Fotocollectie Anefo, 1971, W. Punt, Nationaal Archief

As evening fell, cars would depart one by one. Eventually, both the back areas and the shopping alleys would become fully deserted. I cherished this moment, as both contrasting spaces would eventually blend into one — a quiet and closed shopping centre. As darkness enveloped the outside and our studio glowed, being the only illuminated space, the sticker proved less effective as light seeped through. The studio then transformed into a massive light box, ultimately exposing our lonely indecent working hours.

The Dark Store

After almost two years, our studio was rented out to become a cosmetic salon. We were evicted and relocated to another nearby empty store, this time a former Dynabyte, a Dutch retail chain of computer-related products and services that declared bankruptcy in 2015. We were displaced to make room for beauty enhancement services like hair laser removal, tattooed makeup, and temporary lip thickening; to finally find ourselves replacing the obsolete hardware of the computer era.

After a mere six months in this new studio, we faced eviction again, this time with no alternative space available. This second studio was rented out for its "real" market value to Getir, an online grocery service promising delivery to your home in just 10 minutes. Consequently, they operated in what is known as a dark store: a warehouse with shelved products ready for dispatch.

Dark stores alter our perception of traditional shops, as their windows are closed off, and products come and go through the back door. They utilise space purely for its functionality, serving as storage capacity. They need to be strategically located, close to the city centre for accessibility by delivery drivers. These facilities often repurpose former shops, presenting a minimalistic front with a usually white background and a moderately sized brand logo. However, as these dark stores popped up across the city, the consumers of the urban landscape have started missing the visual stimulation provided by displays and advertisements. Cities then began regulating the establishment of new dark stores due to their impact on the visual aesthetics of a neighbourhood. In response, the on-demand grocery service companies started showcasing art on their windows, transforming into gallery fronts that disguised their actual dark operational activities — reminiscent of that sticker hiding our artistic activities, as they did not conform to the shopping centre's rules of beauty.

*

Today, I recall with nostalgia those two studios that were so spacious and affordable. They were places where I could make noise, engage in messy work, and host parties that spilled into the back parking lot. It felt like being hidden, carrying all the potential that entails, and perhaps that's exactly what we were — situated at the margins of the city, in a temporary non-place, and ousted when it regained monetary value. It was momentarily convenient for all.

In a similar way, the shopping centre was built on a promise and already inaugurated as a ruin. It was constructed to unite a suburban community with shopping and leisure options. However, like some other shopping centres from their very opening, it failed to meet the utopian expectations while requiring endless replanning.

I like contemplating spaces that can either be realms of consumption or production. As artists, we often find ourselves treated as products to be consumed. Navigating through back doors, we hide when necessary or emerge to entertain at the opportune moment.

This story is one of many. A city shapes our artistic practice and spaces are being constantly redefined. And in this case, the shopping centre serves as an experiment for a micro-society to coexist, play, entertain, stumble and sometimes fall.

Buikslotermeerplein, Collectie Archief van de Dienst Ruimtelijke, 1979, Stadsarchief Amsterdam

Products & Services

16 labels:
8 fragile
4 x airmail
4 x urgent
22 pieces:
60 pieces
Weight: 5 kilos
100ml
And more!
See inside
Semi
Tm
Ce
Ltd
R
Pefc

Bag and Bootleg

Elaine M L Tam

{Prelude}

We shall only attribute energy towards getting serious about the frivolous things, be they as small as a choice of frill, button, or any other form of minor detailing, or as big as the fate of the half-shuttered *99c Paradise* across the road that, relegated to the limbo-land between closing and opening, persists in spite of everything. To aid our appraisal, we have identified the 'bag' and the 'bootleg' as two interlaced domains of operation; to valorise and champion frivolity — an otherwise disqualified *aesthetic* mode — shall be our primary occupation.

{Enter: 'Bag Lady'}[1]

She's a nail-biting, streetwalking, bag-slinging bad-ass.[2] Sometime in the distant past, a mother teaches her daughter that she has the license to snap back: 'never look in a 'lady's' handbag'. It is shrugged off the shoulder as if it were a universally accepted defence statement. [See: bag-as-home: as interiority, a living archive, hideout or sanctuary, *a room of one's own* when — pushed out to the hostile fold of the world with the startled morning — you might otherwise have none.] Only part understanding what appeared either too useless or cryptic to be a sound piece of advice, she feels the prick of a faint indignation, stumbling at the first hurdle: but what if I'm not even a woman, much less a lady?[3]

For now, let's go back to the bag. *If* tools become her, the bag speaks of a multi-directional, anatomical feedback loop: she takes shape along its stitching, along the beautifully articulated lines of a well-trained actress, a simple masterpiece wrought with care.[4] Fray with the fabric of its slack lining, your emotive flesh sack! Through this text, she surrenders her hide, we tally the contents of her bag like a listed confession. She volunteers before I even ask, (as offering, as demonstration, as plight), *oh! the lengths one will go* to show that we endure but we are not invulnerable. In earnest, I offer you her script, tentatively she unzips…

Here, everything is talismanic *objet trouvé*, words called to performance with footnotes stuffed in so many pockets, forget-me-nots, precious stowaways. The contents of this bag serve one or many of the following {1} 'to have and to hold', a revised account of possession {2} enterprising the Self, a parody {3} failsafe, to the aid of a stranger in need.

{Scene 1}
'to have and to hold', a revised account of possession

'You can have anything you want.' As if wanting and having were prised apart in some ancient drama, whose natural destiny is to be reunited, to complete each other. Success is defined by the meeting of these two things, the satisfaction of a perfect resolution. There can be friction and flirtation to arouse want and increase the pleasure of having, but no atonality or minor keys.

From the earliest moment, a fragility, a want of orientation, the anxiety of infinite exposure. Only regression recalls the bag in its adumbrate conception. Imagine, a baby gestated in a monoprint Louis Vuitton in place of an amniotic sac. Imagine! A foetus grown in the thin plastic carrier of an off license, emblazoned with a big yellow smiley and text in serif type: *Thank You.*[5] This holding, or the love of being held, becomes metaphorical psychical space, the therapist explains to Bag Lady, whose fingers are laced in her lap.[6] Elsewhere, a custom size of cellophane wrapping is ordered on demand in bulk — because, economics of scale — and left uncollected to one side of the off-license for a number of years until it is finally thrown away.

Packaging is the viscous ectoplasm of the commodity, it attaches to the product of the self, transmits glow, leaves residue, is the Self dissipating like a tired little haunt.[7] Do a-signifying signs have agency? What to make of a comma longing for syntax; a ruler longing for measure; an artwork bought as an investment sitting in the dark, climate-controlled rooms of a freeport storage, longing to be seen.

She wanders into that startled morning, bag in tow, thoughts like loose ends, reminiscences of home that almost feel like an embrace. Design is a principle that shapes a course of action, such that we say 'by design' to infer some omniscient presence that lies beyond our knowledge or control. No sooner than we revel in the achievement of the 'design' of something — it's elegance, it's facility

---

1. 'Camp sees everything in quotation marks. It's not a lamp but a 'lamp'; not a woman, but a 'woman' [...] Being-as-Playing-a-Role.' Susan Sontag, *Notes on Camp*, 2018, London: Penguin, p.9
2. 'I am an aging, angry woman laying mightily about me with my handbag, fighting hoodlums off. However I don't, nor does anybody else, consider myself heroic for doing so. It's just one of those damned things you have to do in order to be able to go on gathering wild oats and telling stories.' Ursula K. Le Guin, *The Carrier Bag Theory of Fiction*, 2019, London: Ignota Books, p.33
3. Echoes Simone de Beauvoir's assertion 'one is not born, but rather becomes, a woman.' And, with more currency, the positing of the question: 'If we refuse to become women, we might ask, what happens to feminism?' Jack Halberstam, *The Queer Art of Failure*, 2011, Durham: Duke University Press, p.126
4. Artistic practice involves rehearsal, after all.
5. A mother holds, she weathers, 'insulating the infant in his state of 'going on being' from the relentless, unalterable otherness of time [...]' Thomas H. Ogden, 'On holding and containing, being and dreaming', 2004, *The International Journal of Psychoanalysis*, 85 (6), pp.1349–64
6. Following Donald Winnicott's thought that 'One of these later forms of holding involves the provision of a 'place' (psychological state) in which the infant (or patient) may gather himself together.' Ibid.
7. 'residue is a way of haunting the commodity. Detritus is the opposite of the commodified object—new, sleek, just off the assembly line, already losing its value as we walk out the store.' Patricia Yaeger, 'The Death of Nature and the Apotheosis of Trash; or, Rubbish Ecology', 2008, *PMLA*, 123 (2), no.2, pp.321–39

Products & Services

— it is left to entropy, to thwart, pervert, squander. A jangle of loose change in hand, drawing long or short straws.

A child grows up and learns to shed selves with the same rapacity as seasons or trends, as casual as snakeskin, they fashion a designer Self. The 'exotics' section before it all became terribly uncouth, I was clasped tightly to her perfumed shadow and together we drifted the labyrinthine department store, looking, desiring. All that *not-having* a dizzying delight so close to the strange bodily affects of falling in love. When all is said and done, 'Bag Lady' once asserted, I will *opt out*. As if it could be so easy: to untick the box in one's marketing preferences. 'To give up' is, to yield, surrender, forfeit control or possession. But it still involves the imperative 'to give'.

{Scene 2}
enterprising the Self, a parody

'Laughter is the shortest distance between two people', she recalls reading from a bookmark that had stolen away onto the floor of the train station. Movement was falling everywhere in the manner of a hailstorm, though there were moments of crystallisation that revealed a larger machinery at work. Timekeeping, the transiting mobs shifted to the instructions of the speakers, faces coming in and out of focus.

Between bootleg artist and 'serious business', there are so many new forms of capital and exploitation – financial, social, transactions in the attention economy, zero-hour contract gigs for employers in niche markets. Time may well be the last reserve of the exploited worker; a secretary steals back hours by daydreaming and writing love letters on company time.[8] The proprietorial self is predicated upon the ability to transform one type of capital into another. I was never good at maths but I can hardly keep track. Counter your imposter syndrome, allegedly: self-commodification, self-indulgence, self-reliance, self-sustainment, self-defeating, self-denying, self-deprecating, self-depreciating, self-conscious. The final stage is a closed loop of autoreferentiality helplessly tethered to itself (and 'I am *so* sick of myself') that reproduces atomisation. Performance turned performance anxiety turned *just anxiety*.

A smatter of lights can be seen through the diamond lattice fencing across a grassy patch fresh with rain. Our anti-heroine 'Bag Lady' walks its perimeter, her thoughts trained on that edge where things fall away and get archived as the past. [See: Lady Jeune's 1896 account of women's entry into retail service at the newly established 'department store': 'Women are so much quicker than men, and they understand so much more readily what other women want. They can fathom the agony of despair as to the arrangement of colours, the alternative trimmings, the duration of a fashion and the depth of a woman's purse.'[9]] Is it really so easy to re-read accounts of history within the framework of queer desire? Can we permit ourselves a strictly positivist reading of woman as a figure of fantasy and seduction? Is transaction not also a form of recognition, requiring empathy?

Improvement is on offer everywhere, perpetually on *Discount!* as the sign exclaims. Can you afford to buy the commodities that signal self-love to sufficiently increase your seeming self-worth to attract a life partner or high-power career? [See *affordances*: the parameters implying a use-scenario for even the simplest work of design.] She responds by releasing the clasp of her purse with a 'clack', manicured fingers studding its equator. She thinks of Walter Benjamin admiring a handsomely dressed sex worker, young Walter with hands dangling from his sleeves 'like receipts'.[10] Because the formula of late capitalism demands we consume and *be* consumed. Because general equivalence reduces time, experience, personhood to its own terms of worth or worthiness.

You can only be exploited if you can be put to use. In a regime where everything can be bought and sold, the failure that marks frivolity can delight by placing one outside that authority or rule. Frivolity is queer and feminist in that it is ticklish; it can mobilise redundancy towards joy, it is ecstasy not excess, it blunders the quantifiable, it hashes the formula.[11] Frivolity in its floundering ineffectuality spawns its very own abundance. (If you have nothing, you can lose nothing, and that generosity of being is a form of winning.)[12]

{Scene 3}
Failsafe, to the aid of a stranger in need

'Bag Lady' martyrs herself for the idea that the purse is the locus of feminine arousal. She is human error; error draws her to the surface, like so many open capillaries maddening beneath the skin. She slinks around the shop windows, and derives enjoyment from the fact that its keepers tense as

---

8   Borrowed from the original '*La perruque* may be as simple a matter as a secretary's writing a love letter on "company time" or as complex as a cabinetmaker's "borrowing" a lathe to make a piece of furniture for his living room.' Michel de Certeau, *The Practice of Everyday Life*, 1980, Berkley: University of California Press, p.25
9   For more, see Katherine Mullen, 'The Ubiquitous Shop-girl', *Working Girls: Fiction, Sexuality and Modernity*, 2016, Oxford: Oxford University Press, pp.97–128
10 From Walter Benjamin's posthumously published *Berlin Childhood around 1900*, as re-quoted in Mica Nava, 'Modernity's Disavowal: Women, the City and the Department Store', The Shopping Experience (ed. Pasi Talk and Colin Campbell), 1997.
11 'Where feminine success is always measured by male standards, and gender failure often means being relieved of the pressure to measure up to patriarchal ideals, not succeeding at womanhood can offer unexpected pleasures.' Jack Halberstam, *The Queer Art of Failure*, 2011, p.4
12 'Waste is, of course, an adjunct of luxury.' Gillian Whiteley, 'Situating Junk: Art, Garbage and Trash Ontologies', *Design, Waste & Dignity* (ed. Maria Cecilia Loschiavo dos Santos), 2011, Sao Paulo: Editora Olhares, pp.129–44

Products & Services

she peers in. They do not know that she looks only at her own wispy figure in the glassy divides, revels in the charged intimacy that the division imparts, feeling (for the first time in a long time) *housed* within a framework begetting neglect and disenfranchisement. Surface tensions betray a discomfit: the bootleg artist looks harder, leans closer, her reflections becoming abstraction until her gaze falls through to the display. In this game of invisibility and transparency, she is a non-sequitur, a shape without form, the part where stitching does not re-meet the other side but instead comes apart.

(In my last session of therapy, I tried to identify when exactly 'dependence' became a dirty word.)[13]

She is something like Levi-Strauss' *bricoleur*,[14] a shape-shifter caregiver versed in combinatorial art forms, a convenor of like and unlike things. Her work is in and of itself a form of reality-testing: in an improvised endeavour, you can only be sure that there is no surety. No divining guide, no didactics, no one solution, no Romantic permanence; she forsakes the authorial original to thwart possession, finds secret loveliness in distributed replication. [See *reality*: a constructed, re-mediated composite – the collision of flotsam and jetsam as unstable images.]

Collage is the uneasy form that alights from the bag and the bootleg. Imperfect suture, it shares affinities with the figure of the artist *bricoleur*, embodies their concerns. They celebrate the signs that cascade by slew and slurry, raining like so many feet of suited businesspeople in the station. If the blistered worldings of postmodern expression issue from the sign's homelessness, collage is that riotous thing of postmodernism. Privileging dispersed fragments over unity, 'collage shows the open mouth, the figure in distress, the scream and its cause; it glues effect to cause and queers the relations between the two.'[15]

To resist fixity is both a trialling work and a work constantly on trial; as a result, the collage must visually, literally and metaphorically contend with contradiction, tension and anachronism. The 'lowly' collage[16] is an exemplary analogy for an ethics regarding the stranger: to hold difference and still differentiate; to love with passionate detachment; to be together apart; to give without expectation of reciprocation; eye contact replacing paper contracts. A commitment to care in the absence of break clauses, failsafes, cost-benefit analyses, purpose-led production, terms and conditions.

I knew you as a child, a third of your years young, my arm span hardly wrapping the width of your waist. You, a vision amidst the curb side maelstrom, detritus whirling breathlessly in uneven wind. Hand in pockets, in bag, you stir, with the agitation of the coven's brew. I waited with eyes like little dog bowls, would it this time be vivid boiled sweet, a stubby pencil flaking its red, or a cranky aluminium tube, rolled at one end.[17] The small big-ness of needing and providing before wanting and having. The world offers itself up in the vernacular of everyday gestures, a gift from the unstable amalgam of her bag.[18]

{Closing scene}
Frayed ends

The appropriation of a woman's love has first entailed turning her care into a matter of frivolity. Slung over the shoulder is this handbag of feminist contentions: maintenance against planned obsolescence; gestation (or *holding*) against unwaged care work; acts of service against servitude. [See 'a labour of love': towards social reproduction.][19]

Frivolity is risky enough to be earnest, as arbiter, translative medium, thought experiment, protector of minor things. Is it true: all a crossing takes is a bag? When you have but few things left but the comfort of strangers. She makes do because she is homemaker – she does not build up but around, she pads out problems, she sidles forth, she scribbles in the margins, she gets words in edgeways.[20] Maybe she's done 'dealing with it', hanging on, barely or *just*. Or maybe 'getting by' for now means laughing it off, with a plan in mind.

And yet stood in the aisle of the *99c Paradise* clutching marigold-coloured rubber gloves presented in a 'saver's pack' of three, her inclination is to contemplate them a moment longer. With her adeptness in niceties and platitudes, she might occasionally overcome the dominance of the sign for a love of the webbed relations that constitute it. She walks out into another startled morning being all the women she could have otherwise been (or in other words, none), wondering if she identifies with the feminine archetype of 'saver'.

---

13 'This is the contradictory principle of our professional lives: dependence is the condition of our autonomy.' Andrea Fraser, 'How to Provide an Artistic Service', October 1994, Vienna: The Depot.
14 'a jack of all trades or a kind of professional do-it-yourself person.' Claude Levi-Strauss, *The Savage Mind*, 1966, Chicago: University of Chicago Press, p.17. Strikethrough is author's own.
15 Jack Halberstam, *The Queer Art of Failure*, 2011, p.44
16 'The man who insists on high and serious pleasures is depriving himself of pleasure; he continually restricts what he can enjoy; in the constant exercise of his good taste he will eventually price himself out of the market, so to speak.' Susan Sontag, *Notes on Camp*, 2018, p.32
17 Nicolas Bourriaud has identified the 'flea market' as an 'omnipresent referent' of postmodernism: 'since the early nineties, the dominant visual model is closer to the open-air market, the bazaar, the souk, a temporary and nomadic gathering of precarious material and products of various provenances…' in *Postproduction*, 2006, London: Sternberg Press.
18 In lieu of coherence and happy endings, we have instead plasticity in art, the destabilisation of objects, representation, meaning. Might this give us hope for a state of affairs re-composed otherwise?
19 'Because we are working for our own satisfaction our labour is supposed to be its own compensation.' Andrea Fraser, 'How to Provide an Artistic Service', 1994
20 Because 'citation is feminist memory', per Sara Ahmed, 'Find Other Killjoys', feministkilljoys.com, posted 31 December 2023, accessed 7 March 2024.

Products & Services

Another fine product
Not actual size
Complies with the Couture Club
Join the Team of Protect What Matters
Be safe be legal
Only for
Half Price
Value
Value for money
Best value
Best deal
Best on the market

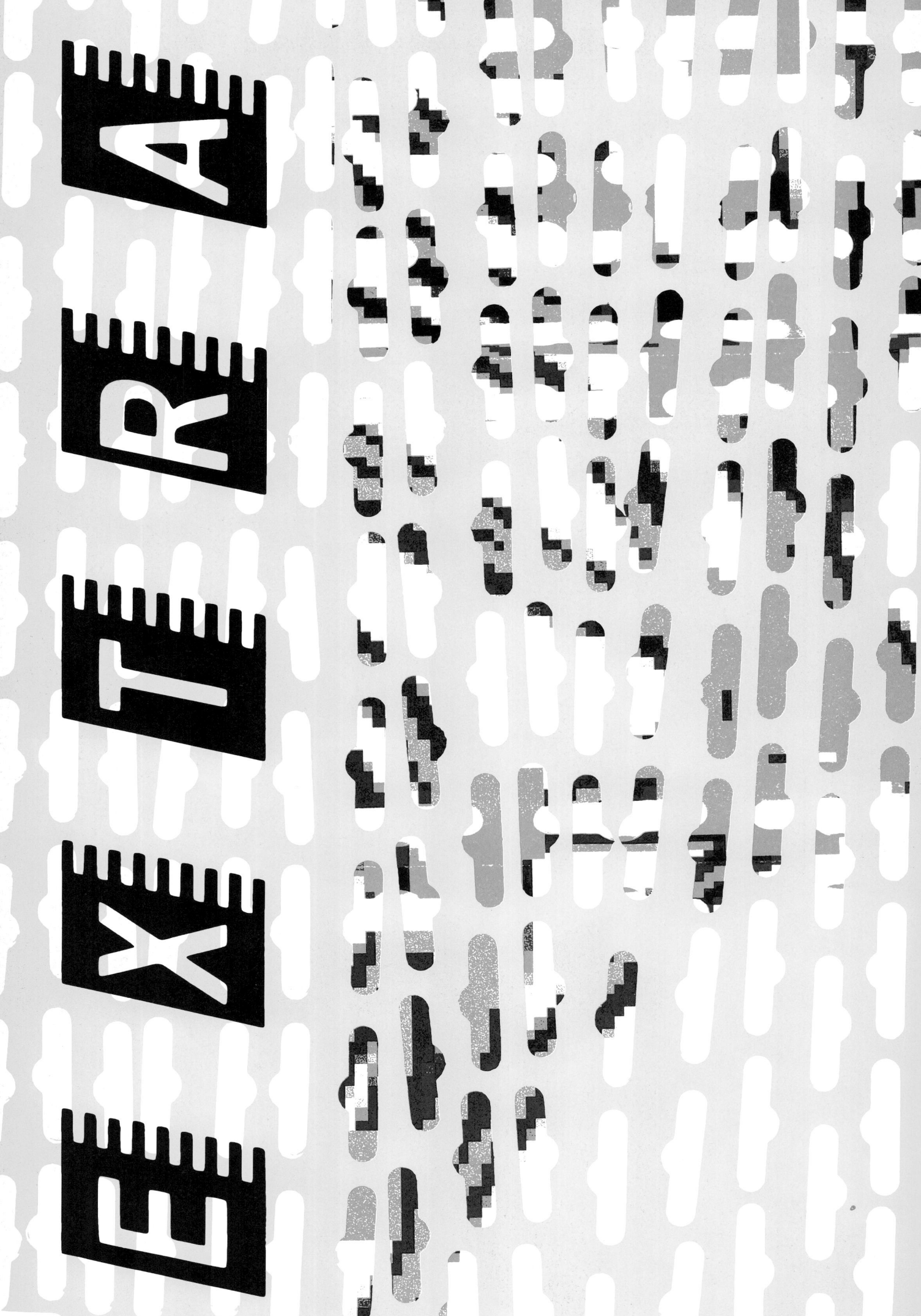

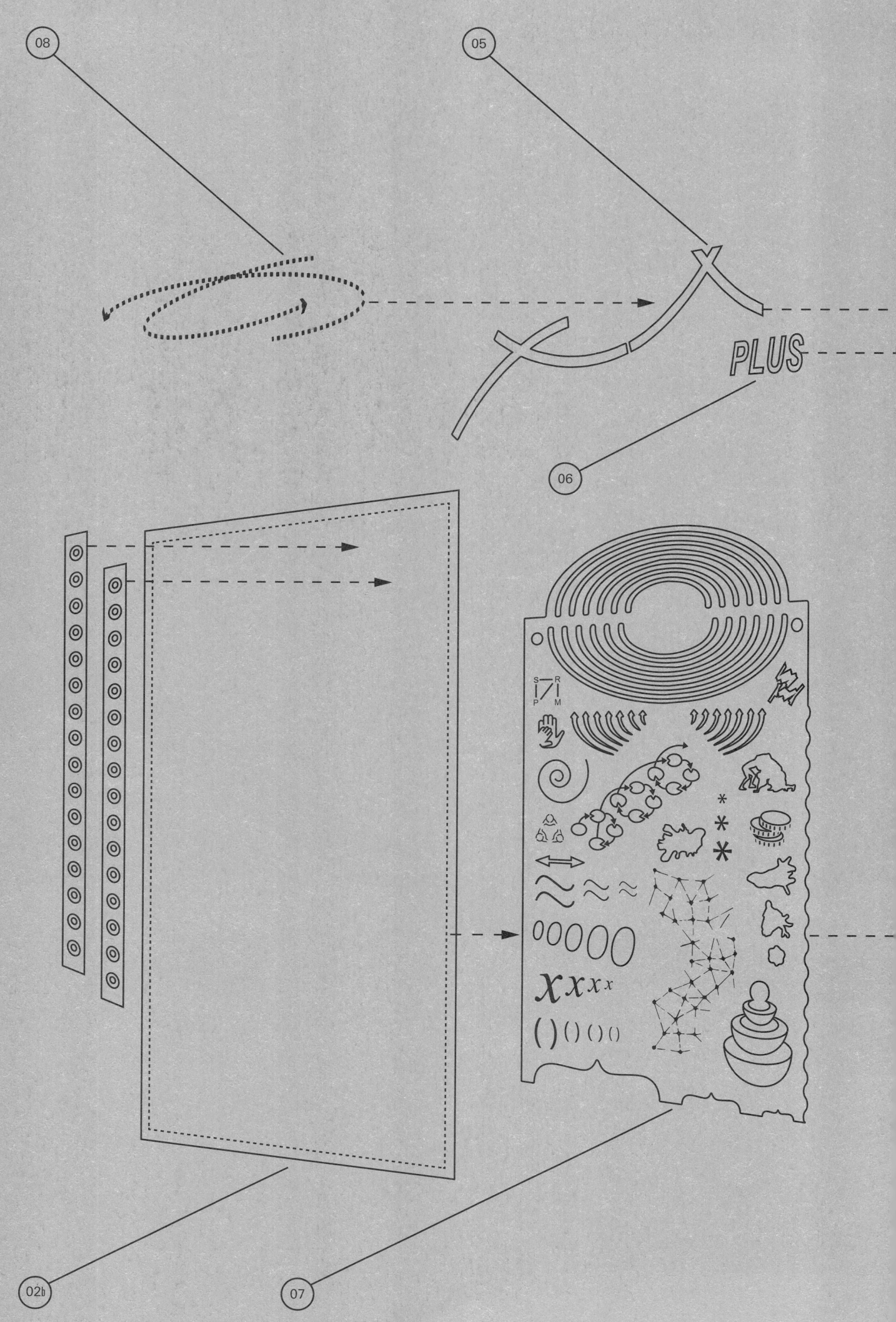

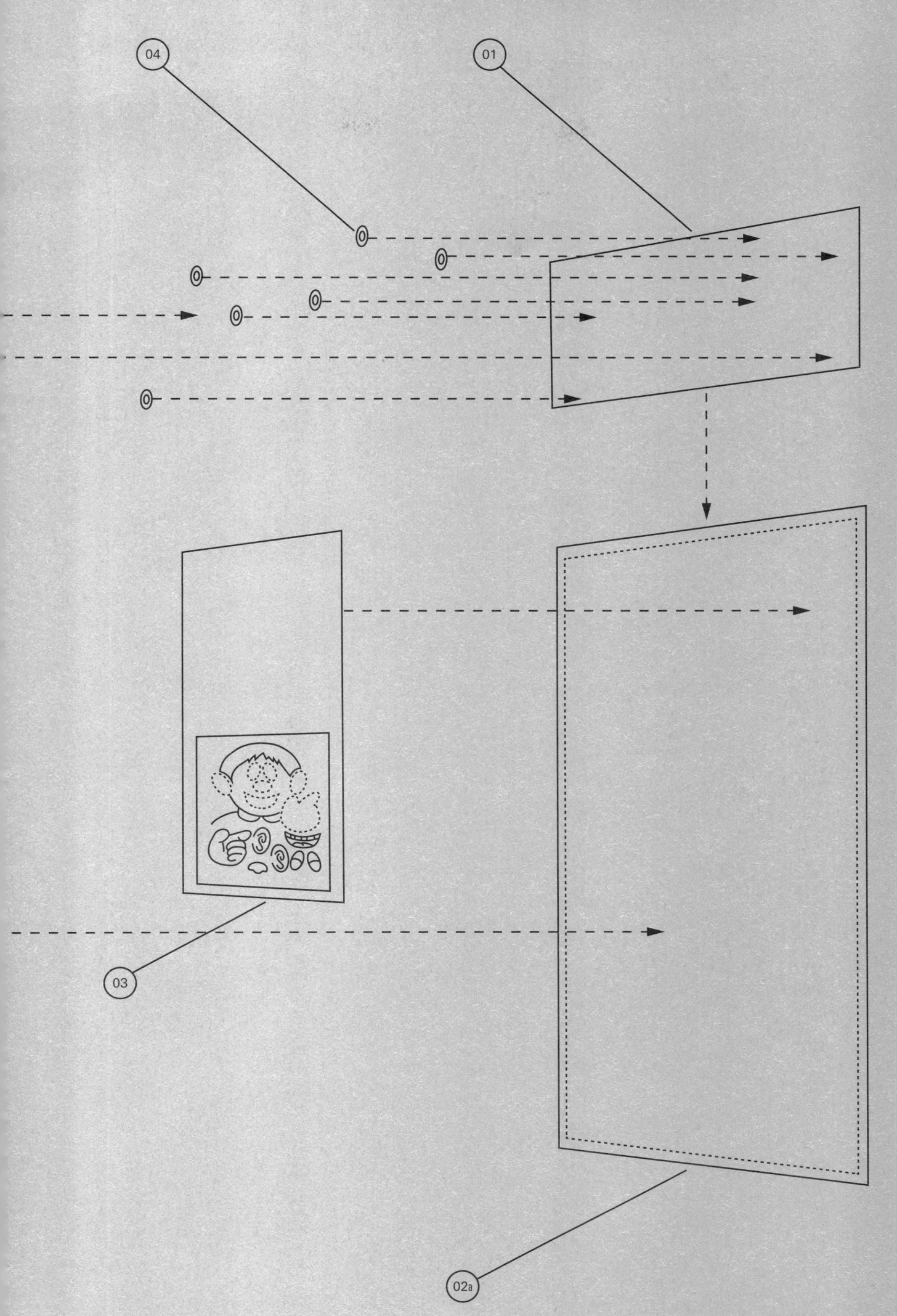

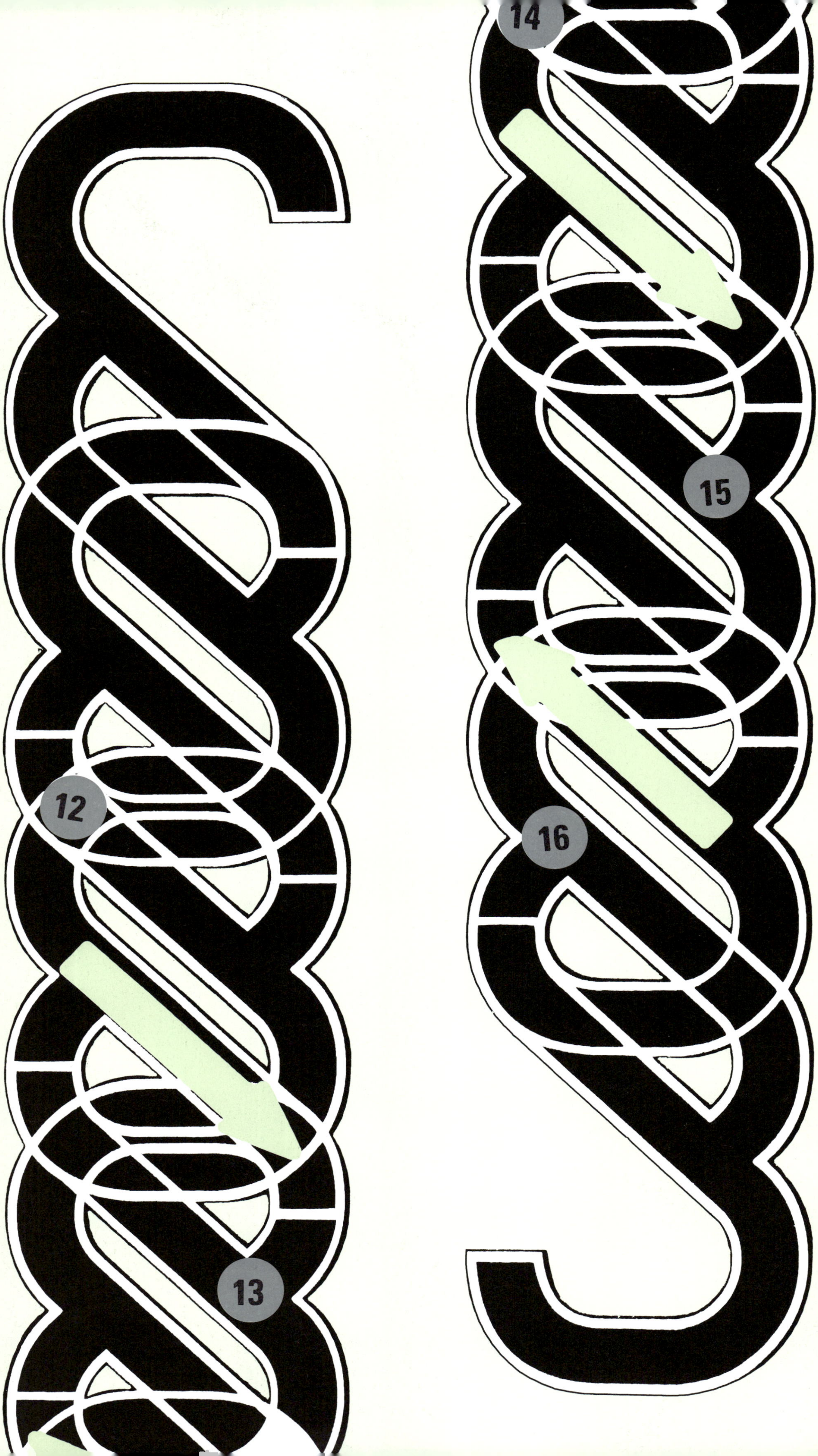

Untitled [While making something else]
(2023)
Poster paper, masking tape
594x743x200mm

(Un)fit for the Job
(2021)
Acrylic, polythene sleeve, screenprint, stickers, vinyl, bar tape, tracing paper, string, hand punched paper, steel
880x360x200mm

Fsiiing for Sale
(2021)
Acrylic, polythene sleeve, screenprint, stickers, vinyl, bar tape, electric tape, string, tracing paper, hand punched paper, steel
850x320x200mm

Originals
(2023)
Plastic, steel, spray paint, vinyl, stickers, sticker paper, paper
700x600x200mm

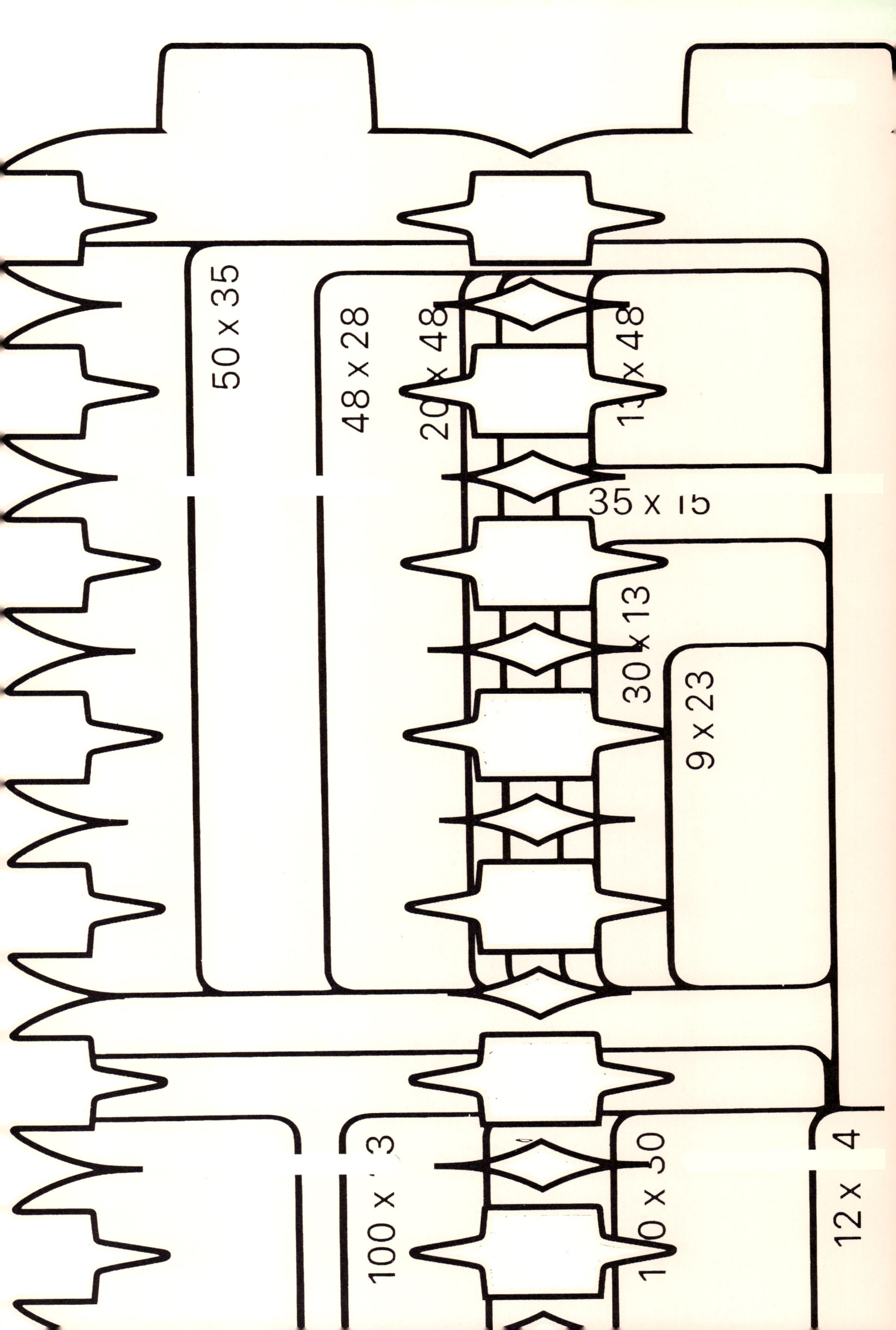

MAJOR VALUE
Helix
INCANTATION PERMANENT
Helix
SINCE 1887
5 Size
3
TIME
1
Helix
INCANTATION PERMANENT
Helix
SINCE 1887
5 Size

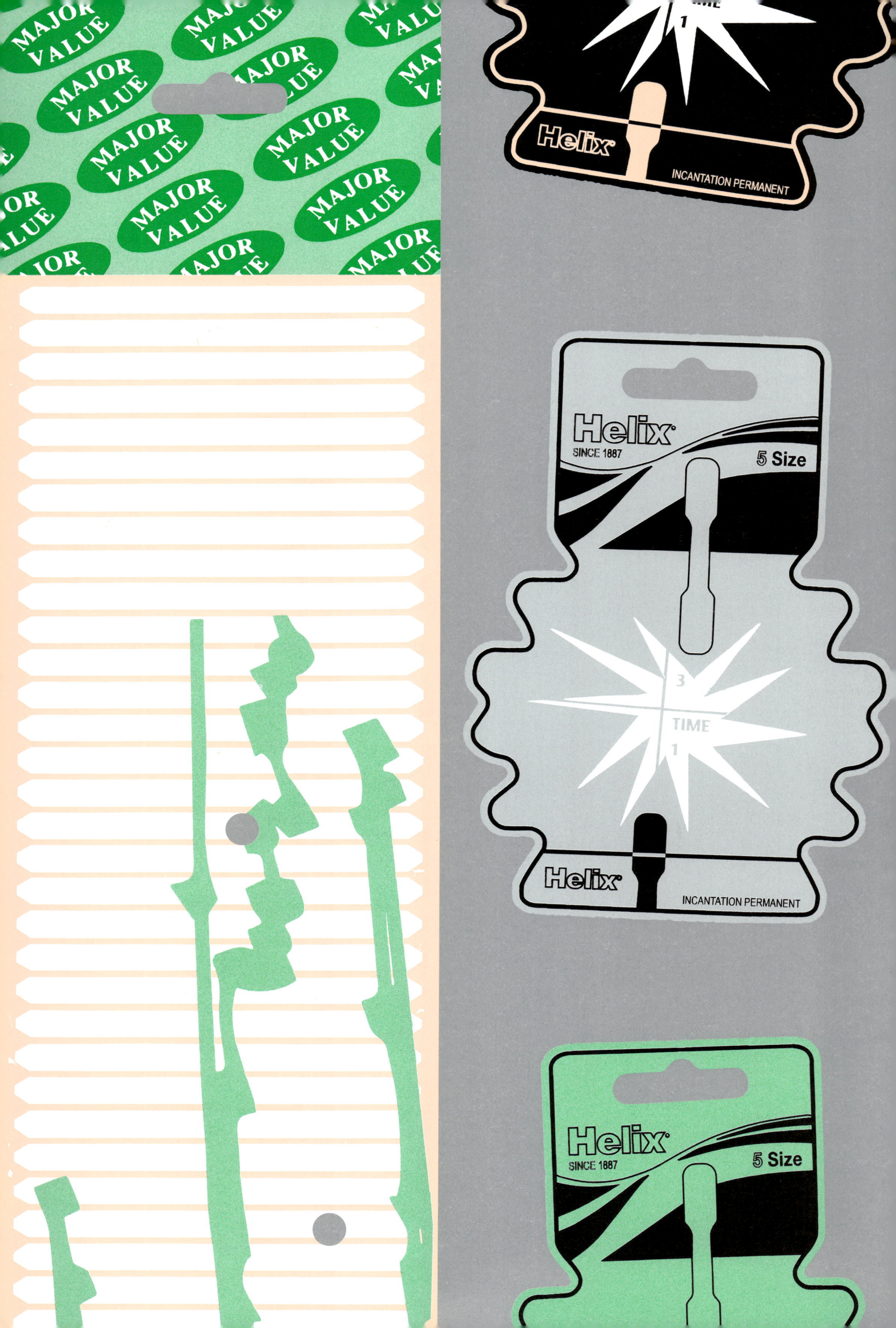

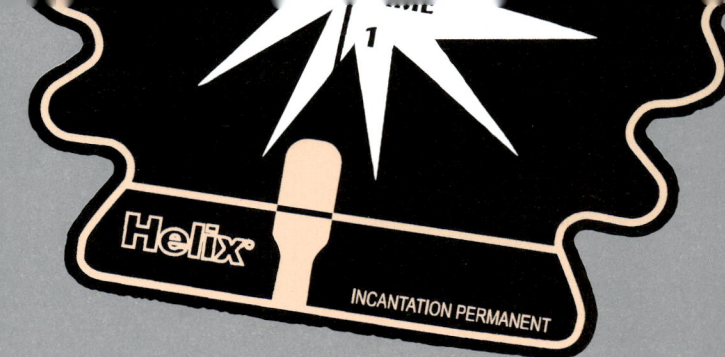

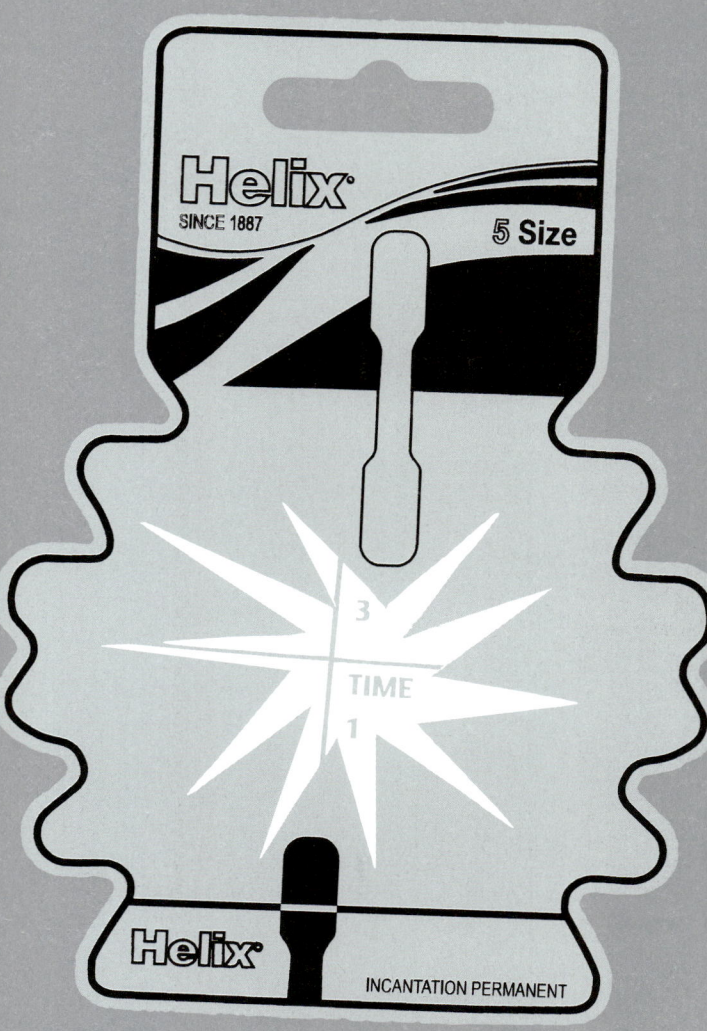

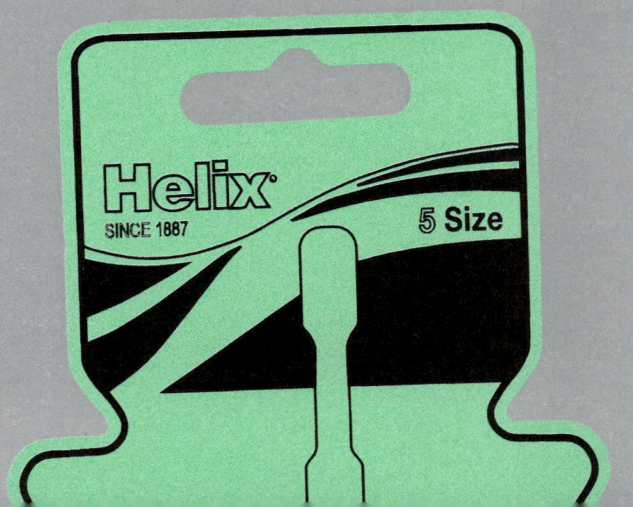

COVER

TABLE 1

TABLE COVER

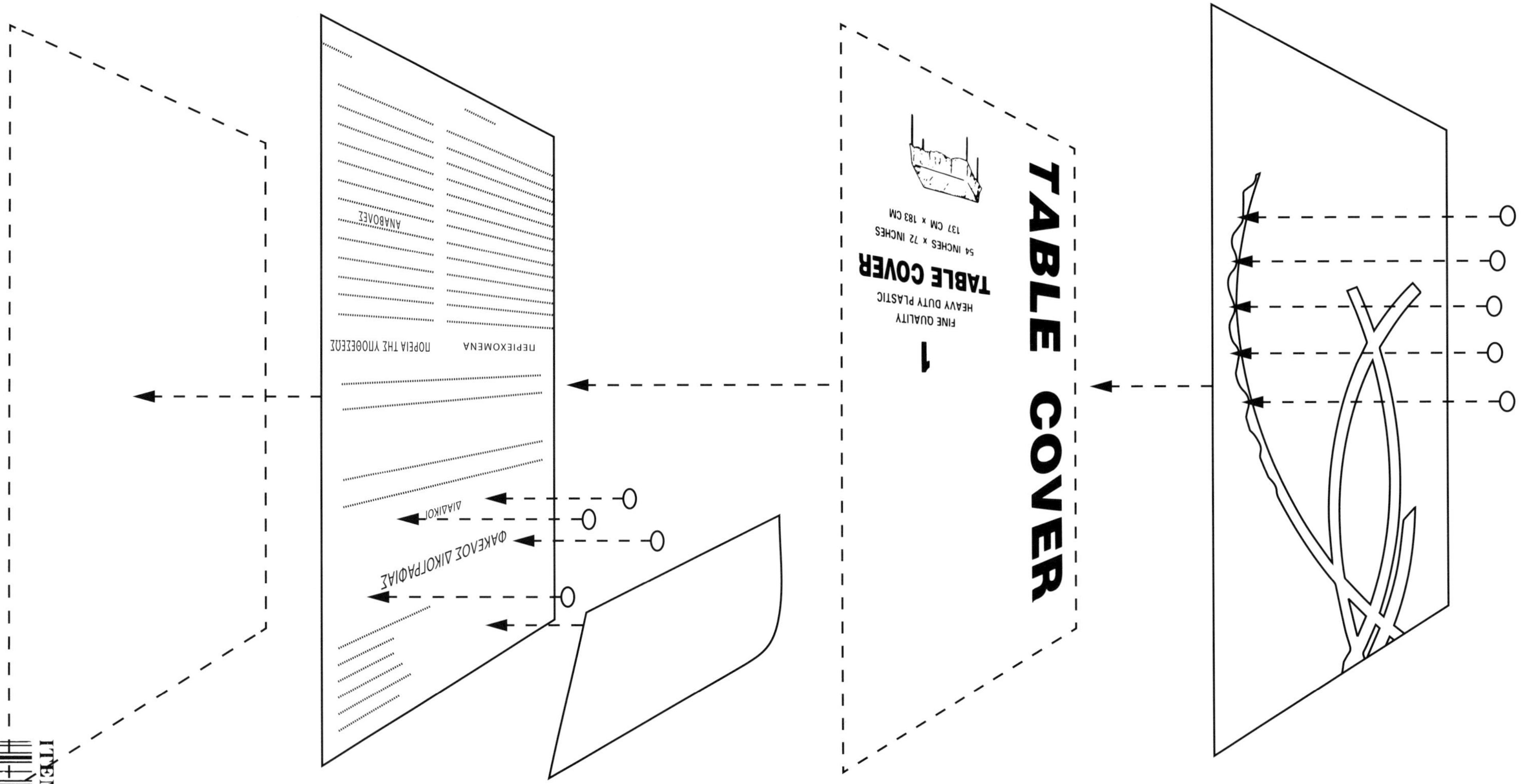

FINE QUALITY
HEAVY DUTY PLASTIC

1
TABLE COVER
FINE QUALITY
HEAVY DUTY PLASTIC
54 INCHES x 72 INCHES
137 CM x 183 CM

ΠΕΡΙΕΧΟΜΕΝΑ
ΦΑΚΕΛΟΣ ΔΙΚΟΓΡΑΦΙΑΣ
ΔΙΑΔΙΚΟΙ
ΠΟΡΕΙΑ ΤΗΣ ΥΠΟΘΕΣΕΩΣ
ΑΝΑΒΟΛΕΣ

ITEM No. JN-10

6 5715 000032

MADE IN CHINA

Fat:	0g
of which saturates:	0g
Carbohydrate:	61g
of which sugars	
Protein:	
Fibre:	
Salt:	

ΗΡΙΟ: ＿＿＿＿＿
ıΜΑ: ＿＿＿＿＿
ΔΙΚΑΣΙΜΟΣ: ＿＿＿＿＿
ΦΥΣΙΣ ΥΠΟΘΕΣΕ＿
ΑΡΙΘ. ΠΙΝΑΚΙΟΥ

● ΦΑΚΕΛ＿Σ ΔΙΚΟΓΡΑ＿ΑΣ ●

● ΔΙΑΔΙΚΟΙ ●

●

ΠΕΡΙΕ＿ ΕΝΑ   ΠΟΡΕΙΑ ΤΗΣ ΥΠΟ＿ΕΣΕ＿

＿ΑΝΑΒΟ＿Σ

ΑΡΙΘΜ. ΒΙΒΛΙΟΥ ΔΙ＿＿ΑΦΩΝ   **54 INCHES x 72 INCHES**   ΑΡΙΘΜ. ΑΡΧΕΙΟΥ

Δημιουργική Πεζογραφία

3. Ἀ. Κοραῆς   Ὁ Παπατρέχας
8. Ἀ. Λασκαράτος   Ἰδοὺ ὁ ἄνθρωπος
13. Ρήγας   Σχολεῖον ντελικάτων ἐραστῶν
17. Στρ. Μυριβήλης   Ὁ Βασίλης ὁ Ἀρβανίτης
29. Ἀ. Παπαδιαμάντης   Αὐτοβιογραφούμενος
38. Γ.Μ. Βιζυηνός   Νεοελληνικὰ Διηγήματα
39. Διήγησις Ἀλεξάνδρου τοῦ Μακεδόνος
40. Ἡ Στρατιωτικὴ Ζωὴ ἐν Ἑλλάδι
53. Κοσμᾶς Πολίτης   Eroica
57. Δ. Βικέλας   Λουκῆς Λάρας

ΕΙΚΟΝΟΓΡΑΦΗΣΗ ΕΞΩΦΥΛΛΟΥ

Ὁ Κοσμάς Πολίτης τὴν ἐποχὴ ποὺ ἔγραψε τὴν *Eroica* (σ. 1).

Ὁ Ἀχιλλέας καὶ ὁ Πάτροκλος στὸν ἀττικὸ ἐρυθρόμορφο κύλικα τοῦ *Ζωγράφου τοῦ Σωσία* (Βερολίνο, Κρατικὸ Μουσεῖο 2278) (σ. 4).

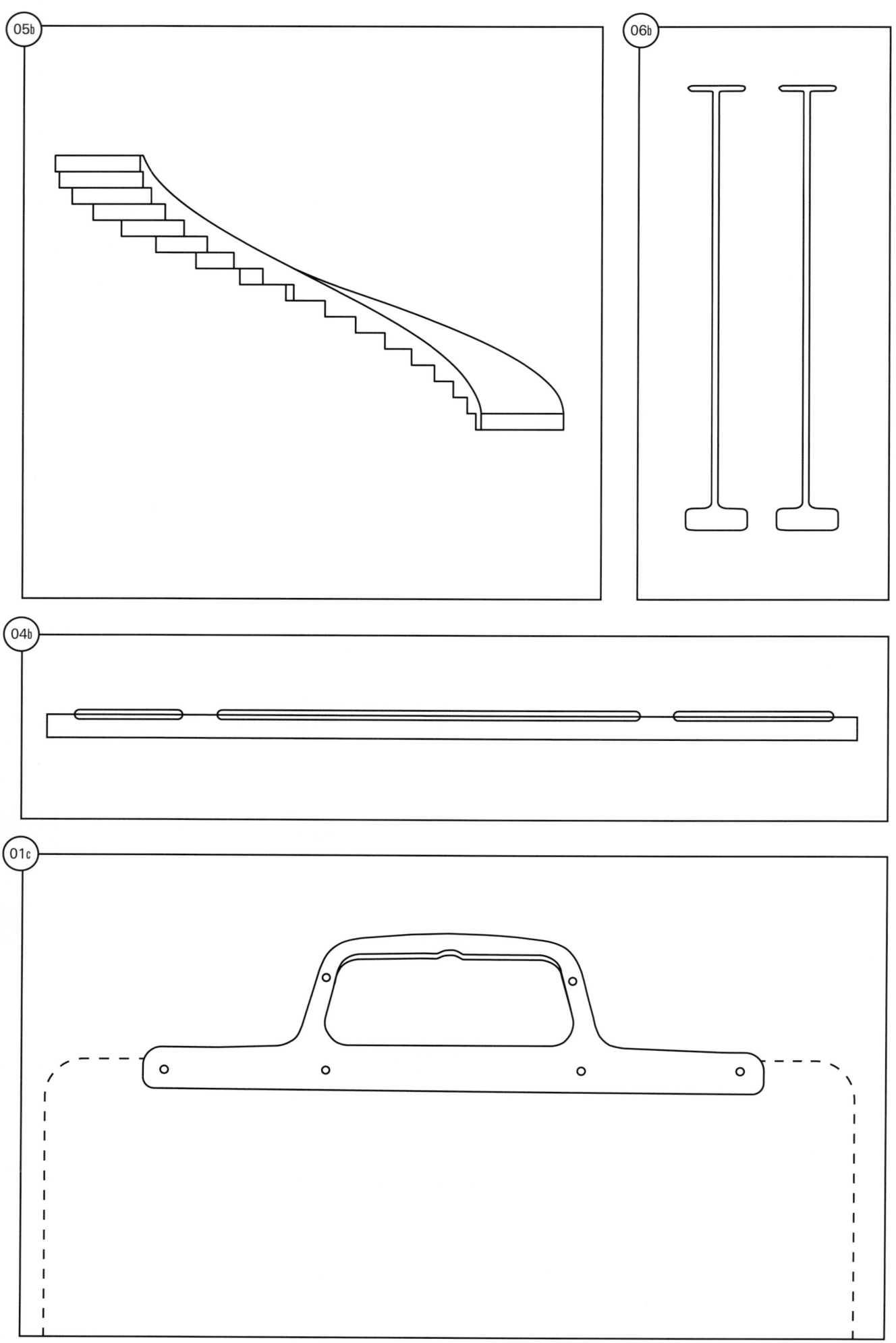

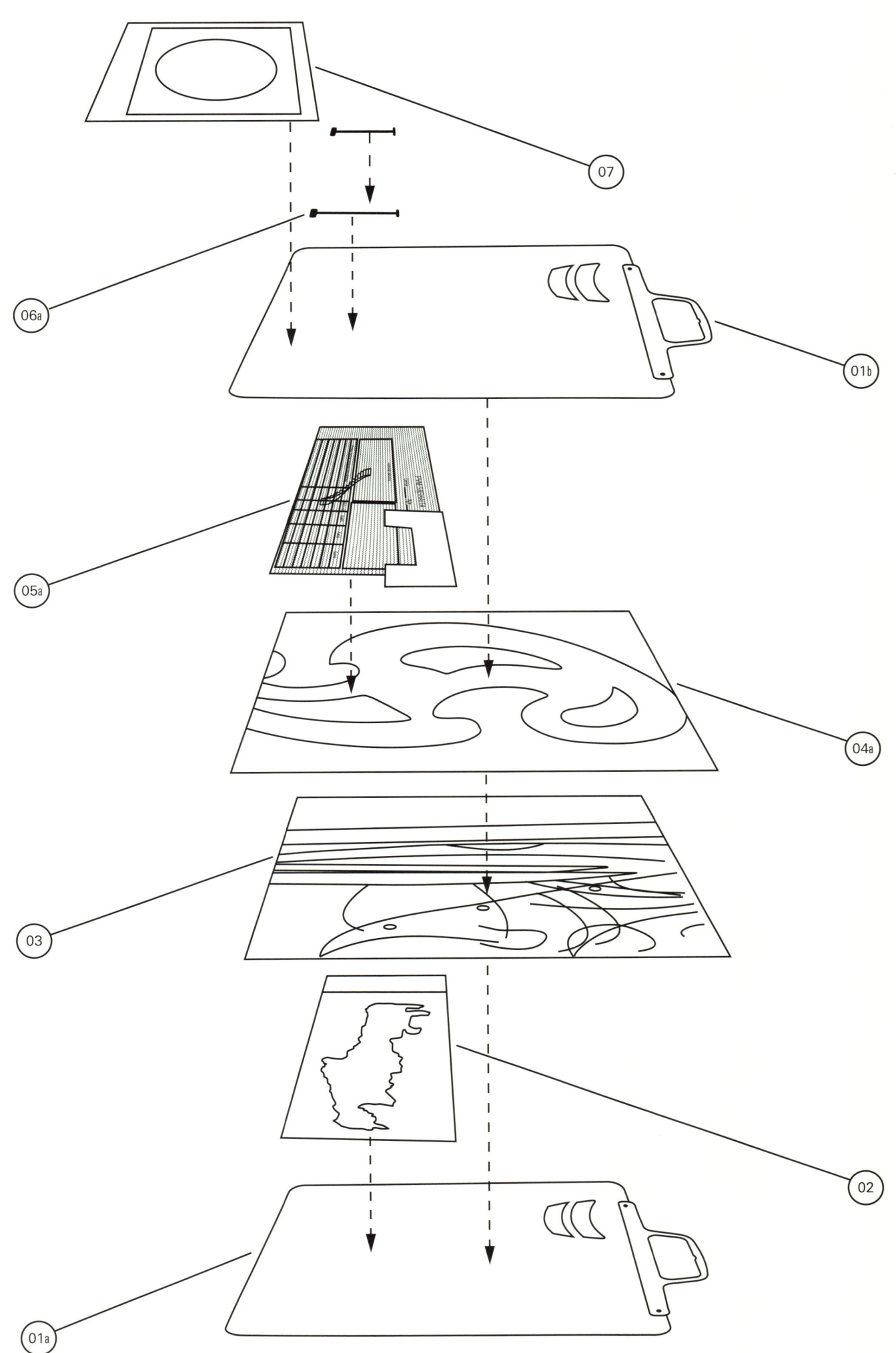

ISBN 960-05-0657-4

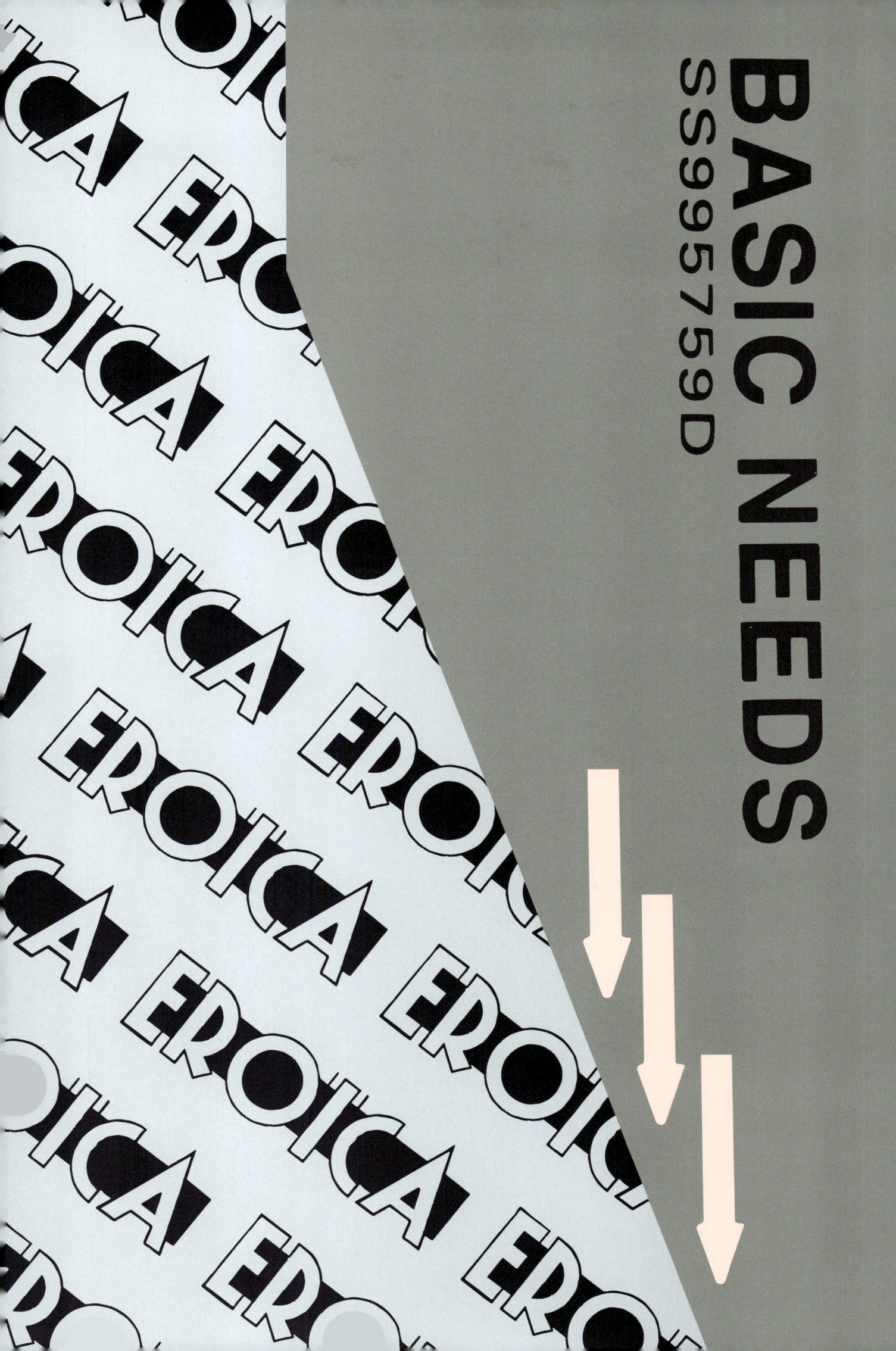

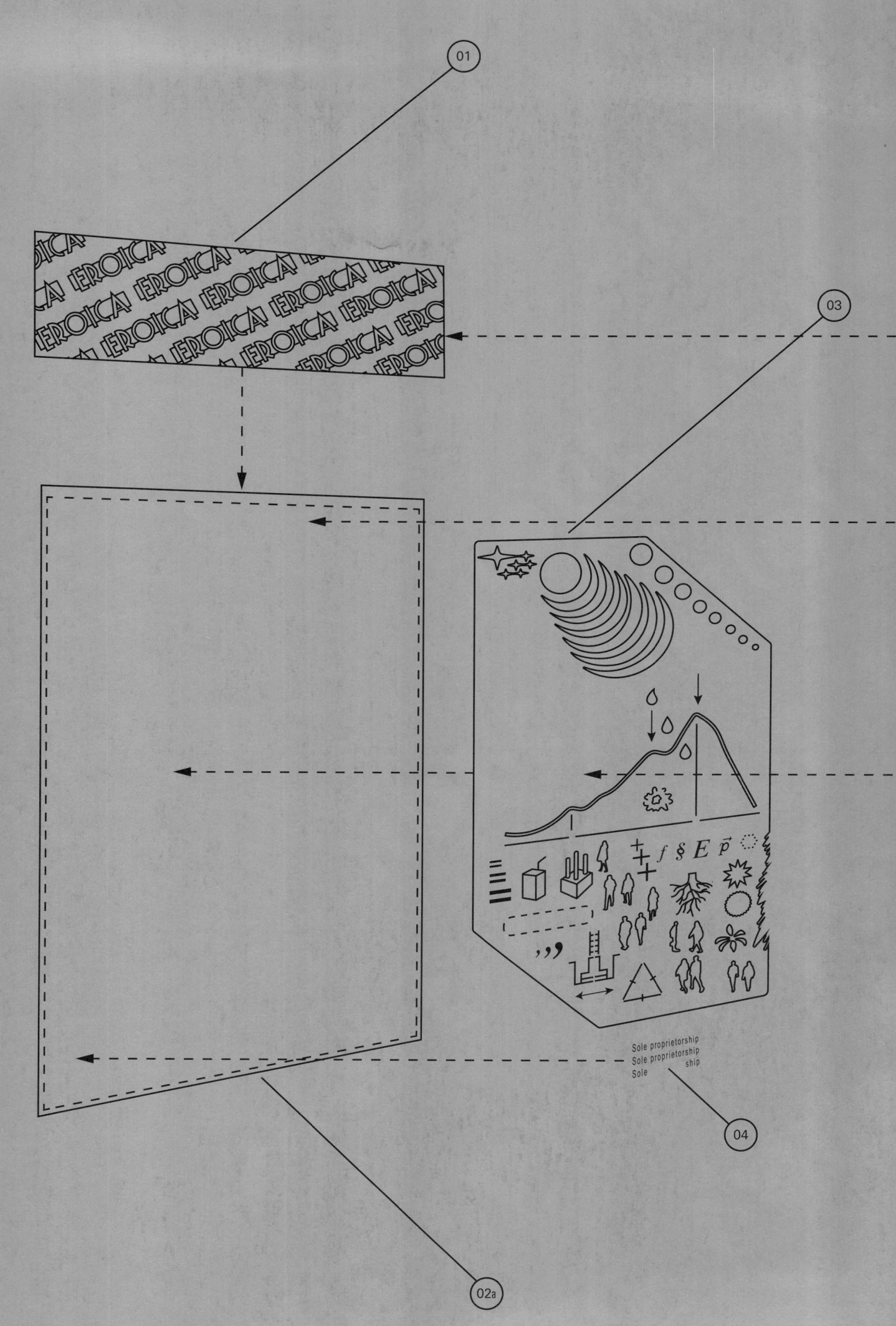

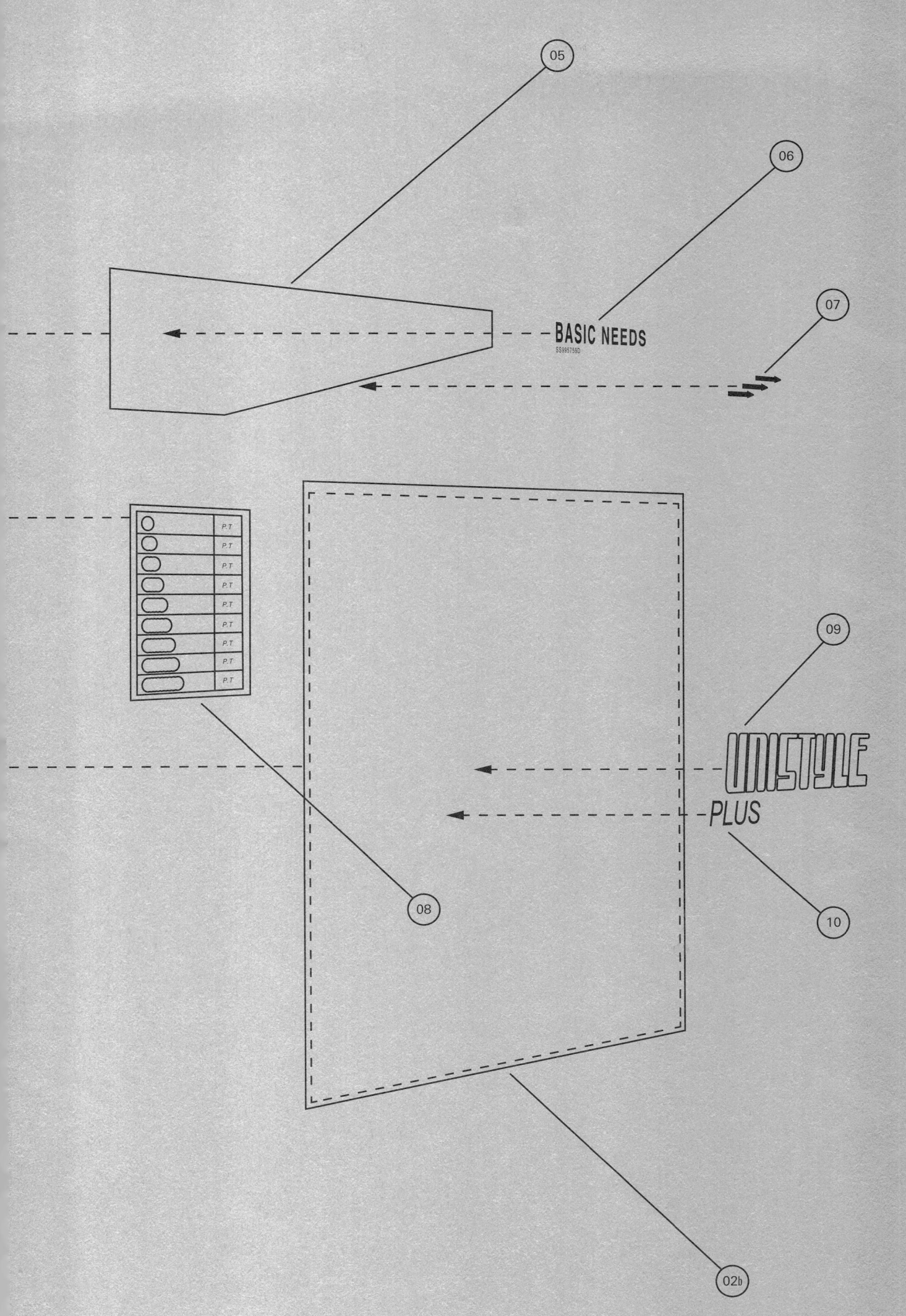

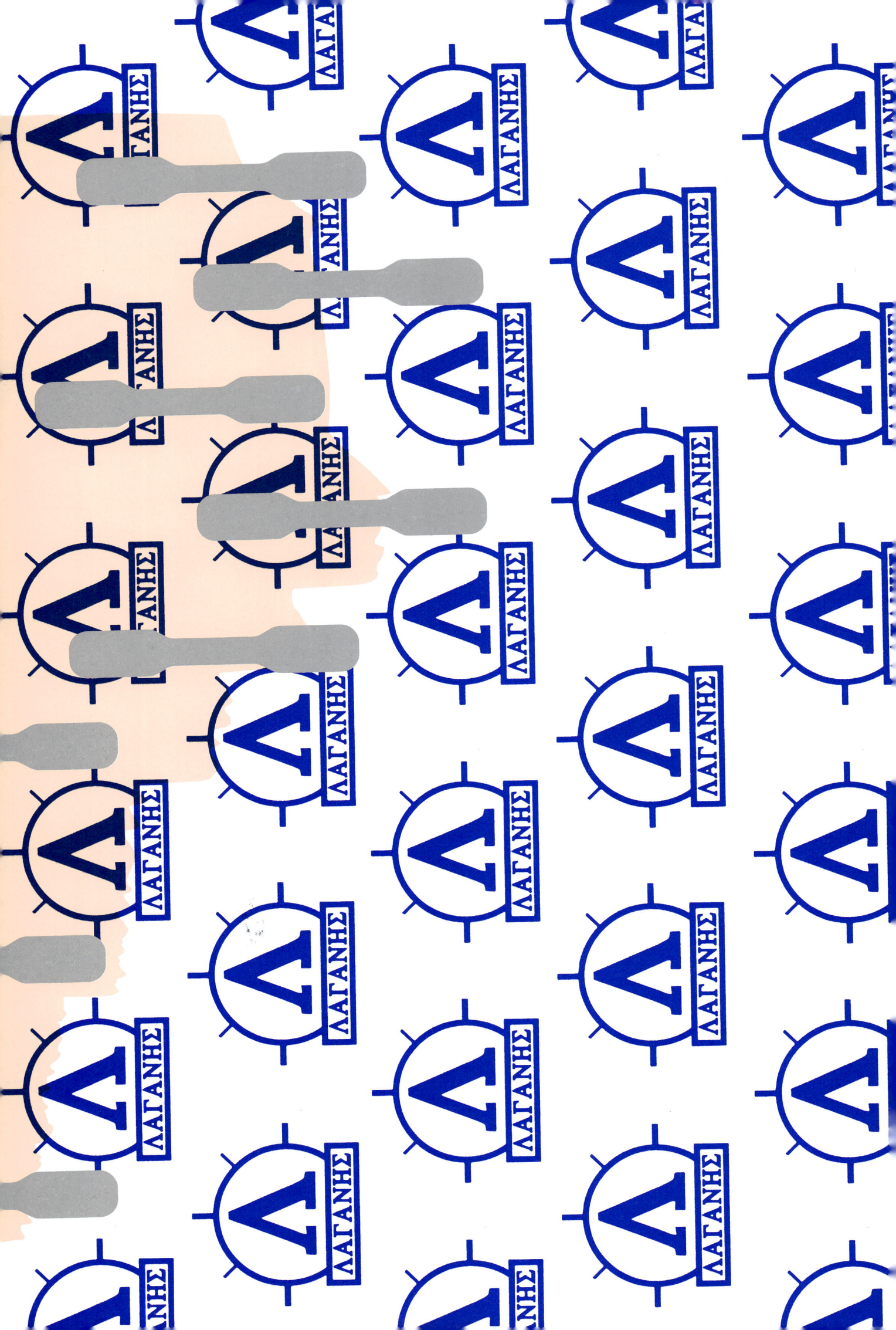

x2
(2021)
acrylic, card, paper, stickers, polythene, plastic sleeve, cable ties, steel, wood flooring underlay
583x851x200mm

X-TRA [1/2 sides]
(2024)
Found polythene bag, black and white print, found packaging, poster paper, tracing paper, jewelery labels, vinyl stickers
100x600x200mm

X-TRA [2/2 sides]
(2024)
Found polythene bag, black and white print, found packaging, poster paper, tracing paper, jewelery labels, vinyl stickers
100x600x200mm

Buy None Get One Free [2]
(2023)
Lasercut card, poster paper, spay paint, screen print, custom stickers, kimble tags, found polythene bag, found stickers
594x841x200mm

KITCHEN TOOL

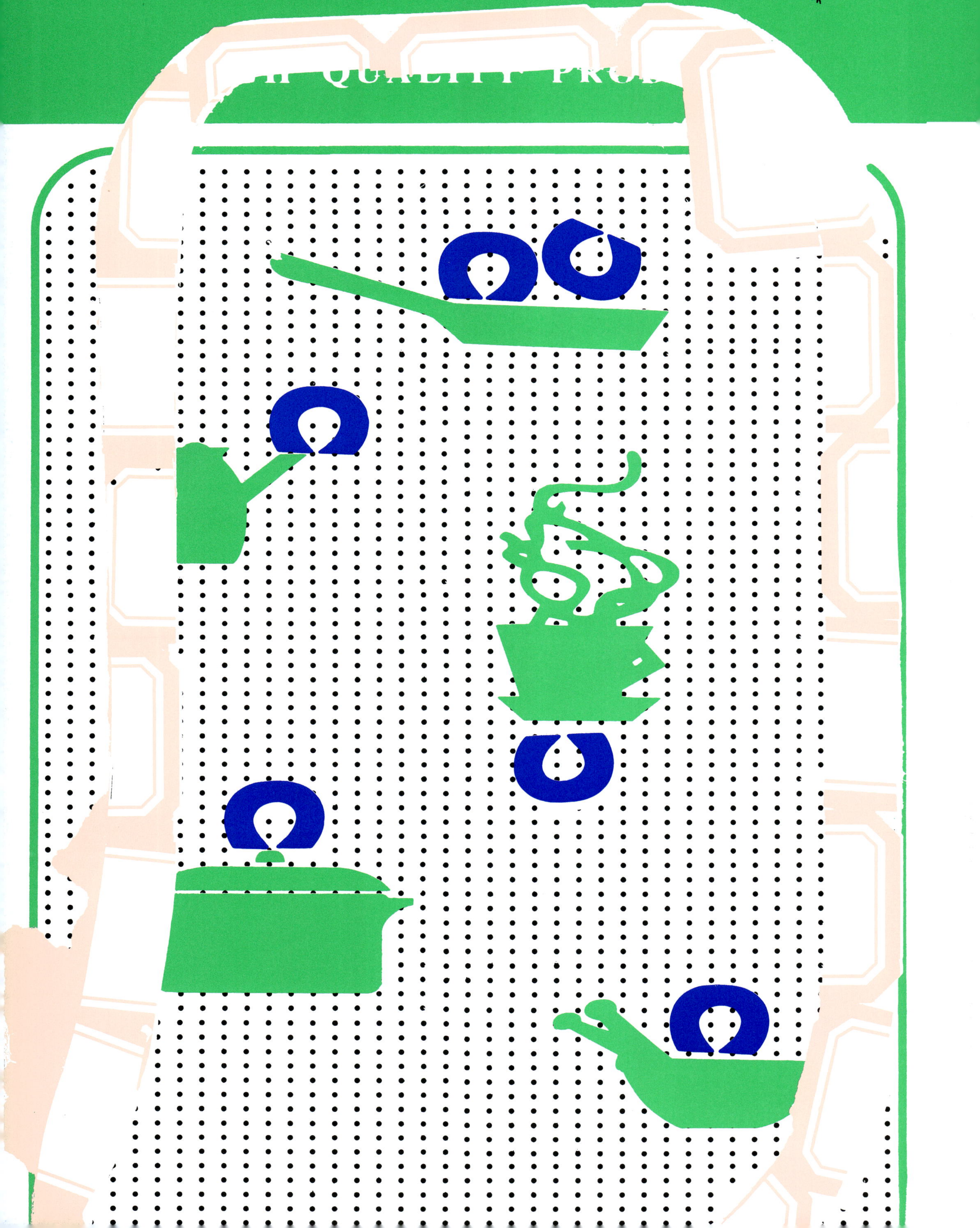

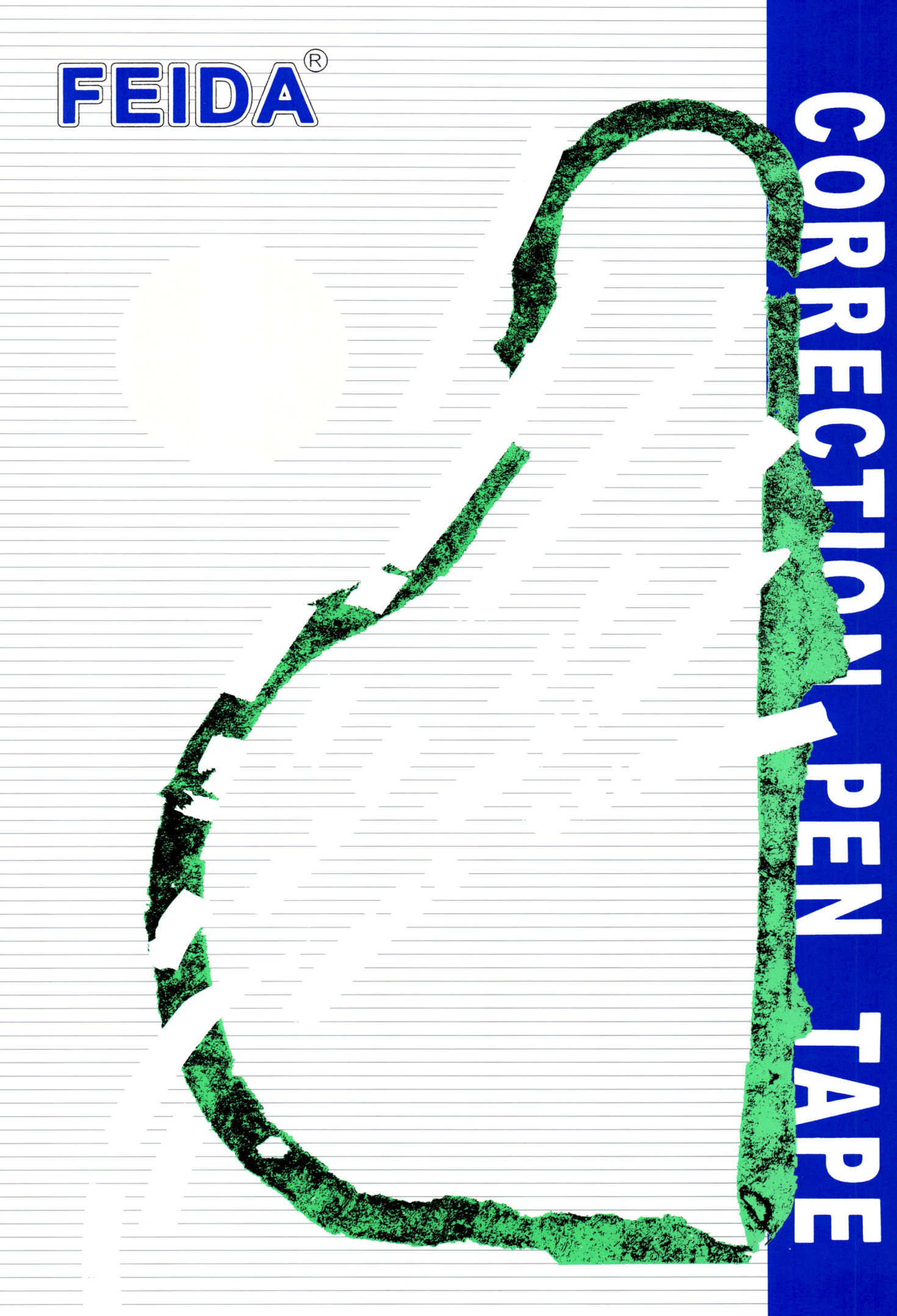

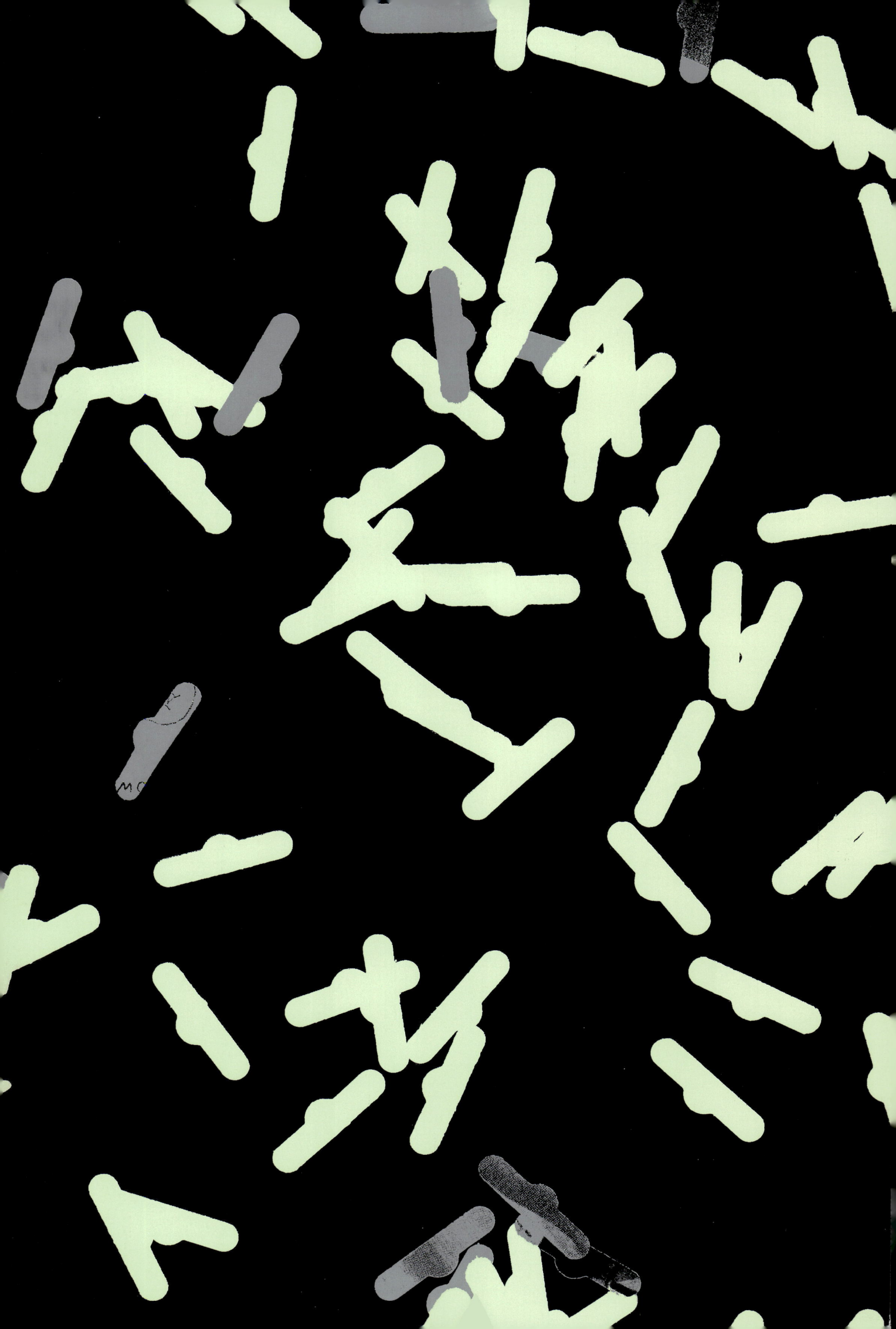

Durable
Distributed
Fit For the Job
get your money back
Lifetime guarantee
Designed for life
Committed
to total quality
Disposable
Precision edge
Precision products
Warning
Sensitive
Smooth
Polished
Protective

Rinse before use
Use & Care
Wringable
Wettable
Scrubbable
Non-scratch
Easy grip
Made to last
Longevity
Power-X Structure
Re-inforced
Hard
Strong
Light
Comfort
Organic

Mega pack
Mega starter pack
Family pack
Ultra large
A pack bundle
40% more
5 pairs / set
Refill
Travel size
Fun size
Mini
Bonus
Included
Increases
Boosts
Tackles

Thank you to Lucy, Lisa & Elaine for their generous written contributions and for having all the right words.

Thank you to Joshua for accepting invitations from the ether and to Sternberg Press for granting permission to reprint an excerpt from his publication *Neomaterialism*.

Thank you to Douglas for photographing my work with so much care.

Thank you to Will for his meticulous design and playful approach.

Thank you to Mireille, Angela, Ian and John for their guidance and for believing in this project.

Thank you to Ashley, Theo, Georgia and Crit Club for their support throughout this process; of amassing, composing and editing. Thank you to all the friends and strangers that have gifted and donated leftovers that have become artwork, and to the friends that have received them.

Lastly, the biggest thank you to Daniel and Foolscap Editions for engaging with my work, for sharing creative obsessions and for the relentless energy and rigour. It has been an honour and a joy to see the workings of your brain.

Supported by the London College of Communication (UAL) Research Funding Award.

ELENI PAPAZOGLOU is an artist and graphic designer, based between London and Athens. Through performance, writing and print, her work explores systems of value and exchange, making alternative propositions about what is worth, who is it for and where is it found. Eleni studied at Camberwell College of Art and the Royal College of Art. She runs the nomadic project space *On Wheels* in collaboration with Rosalind Wilson, and takes on design commissions in collaboration with Ashley Kinnard. She exhibits in self organised and institutional contexts. Recent presentations include *Hole, Hold, Whole*, reclame (2023), *Hall of Mirrors*, PLOP (2023), *Prizing Eccentric Talents*, P.E.T. Projects, *Collective Displays of Affection*, Camden Art Center (2022). Eleni lectures at the London College of Communication [UAL].

LUCY COWLING is an independent curator and contemporary art producer living and working in London. She has programmed exhibitions, performances, workshops and events at organisations including Chisenhale Art Place, DKUK, Goldsmiths CCA, Kunstraum and SEAGER. Together with Mark Couzens she runs Kip, a project space in South London. Since 2018 she has co-directed Against the Run of Play alongside Sophie Bownes and Alice Ongaro. Against the Run of Play commissions artist projects, participatory events and new writing with a focus on female, non-binary and queer engagement with football and sports culture more broadly. Lucy graduated with an MFA in Curating from Goldsmiths University in 2019 and completed a Liberal Arts BA at Amsterdam University College in 2015.

JOSHUA SIMON is a curator and writer. Currently a visiting professor at the Academy of Fine Arts in Vienna, and research fellow at Leuphana University, Germany. Simon is author and editor of several books, among them *Communists Anonymous* (Sternberg Press), *Being Together Precedes Being: A Textbook for The Kids Want Communism* (Archive Books), and *Neomaterialism* (Sternberg Press). His recent exhibitions include "The Dividual" at the Kunstraum of Leuphana University Lüneburg and at LACA - Los Angeles Contemporary Archive (2021-2022), and "Slime" a hybrid exhibition, online and on-site at Secession in Vienna (2024).

LISA SUDHIBHASILP is a visual artist and curator. She develops her work and research around the notion of display and the agency that it generates through design, architecture, and social (infra)structures. She initiated reclame art space, a nomadic advertisement board hosted by local shops that presents practices challenging the culture of advertisement and the notion of merchandise. Sudhibhasilp's work has been shown in different contexts such as art spaces, storage, publications, staircases, art fairs, shop windows, public space, bookshops, offices, museums and stores.

ELAINE M L TAM is a curator and writer from Hong Kong based in London. Tam graduated from Goldsmiths University in 2019, having studied Contemporary Art Theory. She is currently Senior Editor at both White Cube gallery and Fieldnotes, a multi-disciplinary project championing experimental forms and work. Her research interests span queer literature, performative writing, psychoanalysis and new media theory. She has written essays, exhibition texts, poetry and fiction for numerous books and venues, and is co-editor of the art and scholarship anthology *Companion*, published annually.

Products & Services
Eleni Papazoglou

With texts and contributions from Eleni Papazoglou, Lucy Cowling, Joshua Simon, Lisa Sudhibhasilp and Elaine M L Tam.

ALL ORIGINAL ARTWORK by Eleni Papazoglou
EDITED by Daniel Fletcher and Eleni Papazoglou
CREATIVE DIRECTION AND CURATION by Daniel Fletcher
DESIGN by William Lyall
PRODUCTION MANAGEMENT by Foolscap Editions
ARTWORK PHOTOGRAPHY by Douglas Cantor
(pg. 65–68, 89–92)

PG 43–46 THE COMMODITY AND THE EXHIBITION is an excerpt from *Neomaterialism* by Joshua Simon. Copyright © 2013, Joshua Simon, Sternberg Press. Reproduced with kind permission from Joshua Simon and Sternberg Press.

1st Edition of 300
Published by Foolscap Editions, May 2024
©2024 Foolscap Editions, Eleni Papazoglou
except where otherwise noted
ISBN 978-1-7392095-5-1

FOOLSCAP EDITIONS is an independent publisher founded in 2016 that works in close collaboration with artists and institutions to release books and special editions.

foolscap-editions.com

This publication aims to respect copyright and we have followed the principles of Fair Use as defined by the British Library. Please contact the publisher if you find a mistake or see evidence of copyright infringement.

All rights reserved. No parts of this publication may be reproduced or transmitted, in any form or by any means, electronic or mechanical, including photocopying, recording, or any other information storage or retrieval system without prior permission of the publisher.